HENRI RIVIÈRE

HENRI RIVIÈRE

ARMOND FIELDS

INTRODUCTION BY

VICTORIA DAILEY

➔

GIBBS M. SMITH, INC. / PEREGRINE SMITH BOOKS / SALT LAKE CITY / 1983

First edition.

Library of Congress Cataloging in Publication Data

Fields, Armond, 1930–
    Henri Rivière.

    Bibliography: p. 71
    Includes index.
    1. Rivière, Henri, 1864–1951.   2. Artists—France—
Biography.   I. Title.
N6853.R5F53 1983   760'.092'4   83-13841
ISBN 0-87905-133-7

Designed by J. Scott Knudsen

Printed and bound in Japan

Table of Contents

Foreword

Sinclair
Hitchings
Keeper of Prints
Boston Public
Library

Many doors open to us to reveal Paris in the 1890s, a place and time full of experiments, new ideas, and compelling personalities. We return, many of us, artists, writers, historians, and collectors among the number, to draw inspiration. This Paris is not ancient or remote; it is a part of our present.

The door opened to us by Armond Fields reveals human beings, immediate, convincing. It frames a human story very welcome, now that the Montmartre of the nineties, and for that matter the Paris of the nineties, long since have become legends. It brings us human images from the world Rivière shared with Toulouse-Lautrec, Steinlen, Bonnard, and others, images different from those so strongly presented by Lautrec that some are now among the most familiar in Western art.

To all those whose writing touches on Paris in the nineties, the challenge today is to penetrate the legends and reveal humanity. Armond Fields achieves this in a book of fundamental usefulness, indispensable for reference to personalities and movements of the time, but much more a book which will always be read for pleasure and enlightenment. A stimulus to other publication (we can hope, for instance, to see Rivière's memoirs in print), *Henri Rivière* is a revelation of friendships and a chronicle, as well, of the interests and achievements of an artist, writer, and collector.

Is the book, as I seem to suggest, a book about Paris in the nineties? No, it is the discovery—the rediscovery—of a life, lived not in one decade but in eighty-seven years. The nineties, however, lead us to Rivière. He was well known then and for another decade, increasingly less known in the decades that followed, and the phenomenon of the nineties poses a question for his life as for others: what happens to someone who experiences one of the great highs of artistic history, a period of widely shared creativity? Those who ride the high must come down afterwards. While the excitement lasts, some burn themselves out, living to their outermost limits and beyond their physical capacities; they destroy themselves. For others, what follows must always seem a looking-back, a long postscript of memories. Some have the strength, discipline, and wisdom to go on in the building of their lives. The experience of self-destruction was that of Lautrec, the experience of continued building that of Bonnard. Rivière's life cannot be described in terms of so specific a comparison. He was an enduring and resourceful explorer whose humanity becomes more impressive as the years go on. His art, at the same time, becomes more isolated, evolutionary in intent yet attached in style, theme, and outlook to the decades before 1910, when, at forty-six, he was in the middle of his life.

Until Armond Fields's highly concentrated detective work led to the intact, lovingly cared for, but virtually unknown mass of original source material which includes some of Rivière's personal papers and collections and the art of his later years, the artist's story remained full of mystery. He is best known for his prints of the nineties and the decade following. They continue to command both respect and interest. Dealers, collectors, and scholars continue to seek out his work. In recent years, what they learned had curious gaps, and in the years after 1910 they found mostly silence. Now a complete life story is before us. It shows, to me at least, that the keys to Rivière's life lay not only in his articulateness in words and pictorial language, and not only in his rare gift for pursuing his own education, and, further, not only in his enthusiasms and ability to focus intensely on his interests, but especially in his friendships. He consciously sought the sense of shared human interests and comradeship both in knowledge and creation. His associates in the decades 1880-1910 were largely drawn from the world of art; in these decades the stimuli to his own art were greatest. His associates after 1910 were friends who became family. As time went on, this close circle no longer included professional artists. Rivière found deep satisfaction in friendships and family, but artistically, he was left to stimulate and challenge himself. My knowledge of his art in these decades after 1910 is not sufficient to allow more than a speculative and certainly very personal conclusion: that his art retains individuality and character but that his chief contributions to the world of art come from his earlier years when he was so much a part of that world.

The portrait which this book provides introduces us to a gentle man, yet one serious in his enthusiasms and formidable in his powers of study and concentration. He was exacting in his standards. From every indication he was a man of peace, avoided ill will toward others, and harmed no one. He did not seek fame and fortune; he pursued his objectives as ends in themselves. His life was a life of observation, of thought, of study, and of artistic expression. He possessed and cultivated, also, a gift for putting himself in harmony with a succession of friends. For them he felt deep loyalty, genuine affection, and close kinship.

Armond Fields, who pursued his collecting, research, and writing with an intensity and sustained purpose worthy of Rivière, writes, "He has become a good friend of mine, and I share the joy of knowing him." Through this book, we can know him, too.

Preface

Armond
Fields
Los Angeles
1982

Who was Henri Rivière?
I posed this question many times over the past few years—to friends, art historians, and print curators. And in most cases, the answers I received offered little in the way of enlightenment. Of course, we knew his birth and death dates; we knew he was associated with the Chat Noir theater; we knew he was a part of the Japonisme movement; we knew he created woodcuts, lithographs, etchings, and watercolors; we knew he illustrated books; and we knew he lived out the second half of his life, over forty years, in almost total obscurity.

A little over four years ago I saw my first Rivière print. I was immediately attracted to it because of its color, composition, and lithographic technique. While I was able to identify it as a representative piece among late nineteenth-century French printmakers, its features were nonetheless unique. I wanted to know more about the artist and his printing technique.

In four years, my interest in Rivière has turned into a personal quest to know and understand this artist as a man, his creative and personal development through time, his successes and failures, his fame and his influence on those around him, and the aspects of his private life that were so intimately tied to his work.

My initial excursions into the world of Rivière were somewhat frustrating. Yes, there already were some books and articles written about the period in which he worked. Some of these books even included a paragraph about him and showed an occasional representative piece. They might also have indicated his influence on color lithography and Japonisme during this period. Knowledgeable people of the period could offer me no more information than what already appeared in print.

Of interest to me was a book on Rivière, published in 1902, written by Toudouze, which attempted to catalog all of his graphic work up to that point in time. It also pictured many of his works, from early etchings and shadow theater silhouettes to lithographs and watercolors. Unfortunately, only a brief biography of Rivière was included.

My next step was to obtain all of the written material I could find about Rivière and develop a bibliography as a foundation of knowledge about the man. With the help of various libraries around the country, I was able to obtain copies of nearly all of the material published about Rivière. In examining this work, I was struck by the repetitious nature of the information. The material dealt primarily with his work and only minimally with the man and his life. Evaluation of this information did, however, give me further leads to pursue.

These leads took me to France, and Paris in particular. I was able to make some important contacts, people who were able to investigate these leads to determine if any more could be found out about Rivière. Their preliminary efforts indicated that Paris was the place where data about the artist would be available, although the amount was unknown. I decided that I had to go to Paris to find out, firsthand, what I could about him. Maybe it would do nothing more than prove that he was an obscure artist; maybe it would reveal a comprehensive profile of him.

My trip to Paris in October 1981 was an investigator's dream. I discovered a wealth of information, new leads that turned into gems, people to interview who knew Rivière, examples of his works from all stages of his career, insights into his thinking and creativity, and most surprisingly, his own memoirs.

I was able to collect what I sought—and with that accomplishment I can now detail a picture of Henri Rivière. I can now answer most of the questions I have had about this man. And I can now tell others about him, too.

Acknowledgements and thanks are many. A listing cannot do justice to the people who helped me with their interest, friendliness, encouragement, cooperation, and effort. In particular, thanks go to Gabriel Weisberg and

Sinclair Hitchings, whose encouragement pushed me to further research.

To Jean-Claude Romand and François Michel, whose knowledge of Rivière helped me to better understand his work.

To Mme. Geneviève Noufflard and Mme. Henriette Guyloë, whose personal knowledge and love of Rivière allowed them to share all of this with me; my debt to them is immense.

To Marie Leroy-Crevecoeur, a dedicated research colleague and interpreter, whose intelligence, hard work, and sensitivity made my quest a much easier one, my heartfelt gratitude.

To Victoria Dailey, whose editing and expertise of the period helped in focusing the book.

And finally to my wife, Sara, for her enthusiasm, confidence, and tolerance of my work on this project.

Introduction

Victoria Dailey
Los Angeles
1983

Henri Rivière entered the art world during a period of great transitions. Abandoning the confines of any unyielding and stultifying classical, academic tradition, many artists of the nineteenth century experimented with new ideas and techniques with an enthusiasm and vigor that opened the realm of art to entirely new insights and expressions. They ignored the rules that had restricted art to the depiction of classical or religious themes, sentimental, realistic genre and landscape scenes, and portraits of the nobility, military, or haute bourgeoise. The French Impressionists splashed color and light over their canvases with an enthusiasm never before seen in painting. Acceptance by the Academy was no longer important to them. "Art for art's sake" became the motto of the times, superseding and eliminating the idea of art for the sake of religious upliftment, educational improvement, or patriotic fervor. These new views about art naturally coincided with parallel political, social, and scientific movements, all of which toppled the old order and made way for the new theories of Marx, Darwin, and Freud. While there were no major political conflicts in Europe between 1872 and 1914, artistic and intellectual battles were waged which generated the new era of modernism in which art began to explore the subtleties of individual perception and ultimately, explored itself.

Subject matter underwent a great change as artists began to respond to the external influences of foreign cultures and the internal influences of their own subconsciouses. Some artists were absorbed with the idea of returning through art to a pre-industrialized, nonscientific order, to a pure, simple, and genuine society. In England the Pre-Raphaelites favored the art of the Middle Ages as being representative of these ideals, and a major movement was undertaken in which inspiration was drawn from a six-hundred-year-old past. Japanese art was responsible for major changes in Western art as later, African art would be incorporated by the Cubists as the Western viewpoint underwent radical changes. Ethnic arts, particularly Japanese art, had at least been partially known in the West before the nineteenth century, but as were most things outside of Western culture, they were viewed as curiosities. But by the nineteenth century, when ideas of democracy and equality were fermenting and as imperialism brought the products of foreign lands back home, Western minds began to stop judging from an ethnocentric point of view. Other societies came to be regarded as culturally valid and legitimate sources of inspiration. This is in part why the Japanese influence was so pervasive. Artists, as representatives of the vanguard of new thought, reacted without prejudice to Japanese art and saw its inherent beauty and richness.

Japanese art began trickling west after 1854 when the Japanese government signed a treaty with Commodore Perry of the United States Navy agreeing to export to the open market of the West their various goods. What began as a trickle soon became a flood as Japanese prints, fans, kimonos, lacquerware, bronzes, netsukes, and the like were imported in huge amounts to Europe and America. Artists quickly absorbed the new influence offered. There had existed a long tradition of incorporating exoticism in Western art, from the *chinoiserie* of the eighteenth century to the Near Eastern and North African motifs of the Romantic painters of the 1820s and 1830s, but these were mainly decorative incorporations and these influences created little subjective change. Japanese art, though, created a fundamental change, not just a superficial one. Also, the exquisiteness and handcrafted perfection of the Japanese objects contrasted strongly with the cheap, mass-produced articles being turned out in the wake of the Industrial Revolution. Japan, so long hidden and remote, offered a new sensibility to artists rebelling against their industrialized circumstances. Artists, particularly the Impressionists, were struck by the way in which space and form were treated in Japanese art, and they began to apply this new inspiration to their own work. Japanese art opened their eyes to a new type of perspective, so that Western artists no longer felt bound by the classical, one-point perspective system developed during the Renaissance. The scientific rendering of space was no longer dominant as the Japanese two-dimensional, diagonal, and bird's-eye-view perspectives came to be understood and appropriated. By 1872 the critic and artist Philippe Burty had coined the term "Japonisme" to refer to this pervasive influence which had its most notable effect on French art.

Another of the major shifts in attitude was that towards printmaking, which had generally been considered as a stepchild of painting prior to the nineteenth century. Although several important artists had created a major body of printed work (notably Dürer, Rembrandt, and Goya), many artists remained painters only and viewed printmaking as a means of having their paintings reproduced in engraving for mass distribution. Concurrently, printmaking was viewed as a vehicle for social and political commentary in an era before electronic communication. But in the nineteenth century, a movement began to look upon prints as a distinct and separate art form, capable of being admired for its own virtures and merits. The print had come of age. With the exception of Monet, nearly all of the important artists of the late nineteenth century were printmakers: Bonnard, Cassatt, Degas, Gauguin, Lautrec, Manet, Picasso, Pissarro, Renoir, Redon, Signac, Steinlen, Vuillard, Whistler, to cite just a few, and indeed, Lautrec and Whistler are admired mainly for their graphic works. And it was not just the artists of the latter half of the century who created a body of printed works: Blake, Gericault, and Delacroix worked in the beginning of the century; Corot, Daubigny, Millet, and Turner at mid-century all worked significantly in prints.

Socially and politically, prints fit the new democratic ideals of the age wherein art became at least partially accessible to everyone. That there could exist more than one example of a particular image and that that work could still be highly regarded, indeed sought after, was a new breakthrough in how art was viewed. It was no longer the exclusive domain of the rich, who had patronized and supported art for so long. Appreciation and enjoyment of art began to find their places in the new world brought on by the Industrial Revolution.

Aside from changing the makeup of society itself and its need for and appreciation of art, the Industrial Revolution changed the way in which art was produced. A duality took place in the production of printed images. On the one hand technicians flourished as more methods of printing were invented: heliogravure, photogravure, chromotypographie, glyptotypographie, etc. These printed images filled the pages of cheaply produced books which satisfied the needs of the newly educated and literate classes. And on the other hand, artists reacted in horror to this debasement of artistic expression. A movement began to restore printmaking to an original artform, where the "etching revival" was begun in the late 1850s under the guidance of Bracquemond, Legros, Gautier, Baudelaire, and Burty, artists and critics who understood the new need for artists to take up the printed image as a serious and valid means of expression. They saw the decline into which etching had fallen; indeed, it had been virtually ignored for fifty years; and lithography, the wonderful, startling invention of the beginning of the century, had, by mid-century, declined in the hands of the practitioners of the hackneyed and predictable. Through this reexamination of the print, serious artists began to see etchings and lithographs as equal alternatives to painting. The copperplate or stone was as valid a medium as canvas.

The influence from Japan on this surge of printmaking was twofold, for not only did it change the *way* art looked, it changed *what* was expressed. Japanese *ukiyo-e* prints, by their very definition, altered the Western consciousness of art. *Ukiyo-e* means "the floating world," the world of actors, the theater, pleasures, sex, a world rarely depicted seriously in the West. These themes had appeared in Western "popular" prints whose aim was to satisfy the demands of a public not trained in viewing serious art. In the nineteenth century, artists such as Deveria, Maurin, Morlon, and Guérin, names now nearly forgotten, were not considered as serious artists and their works have been largely ignored. But in their depiction of urban life, of urban types, customs, and habits, they showed the "floating world" of the West: the demimonde of Paris, with its sexual intrigue and outlandish manners; the devoted husband cuckolded by a coquettish wife; the country picnic with its festive airs occasionally breaking through the bounds of "decent" behavior; women in various stages of undress. In short, these prints, never considered as "high art," were nineteenth-century mirrors to a somewhat schizophrenic society. Many artists though did see these prints and they became the seeds from which grew great artworks.

Morlon's *Canotiers de la Seine,* 1860, is the popular precursor to Manet's *Dejeuner sur l'herbe,* 1863. Deveria's series on women, *Six Sujects de femmes nues d'apres nature,* 1829, is a forerunner of Manet's *Olympia* of 1865. Yet none of the earlier images caused a stir for they were not created in the context of high art. It was acceptable for Deveria's prints to reach a mass market delighting in seeing itself in a slightly scintillating, erotic manner, but for Manet to use such imagery under the guise of high art was too audacious and brazen for most people to accept. It was akin to the appearance of Pop Art in our own era: how could a soup or beer can be considered as art?

Another valuable lesson learned from Japanese art was that of wit, a striking feature of *ukiyo-e.* At a time when Western art was saturated with expressions of maudlin sentimentality and mawkish emotion, Japanese humor stood out as a source with which to combat this tendency. Humor and wit were incorporated by many artists, and several examples stand out clearly: Degas's *Mary Cassatt at the Louvre,* a very witty portrayal with the artist's back shown to the viewer; Rivière's *Thirty-Six Views of the Eiffel Tower,* witty in its direct conception from Hokusai and in its stylistic derivations; Bonnard's children, often mischievous and impish, mocking the nineteenth century view of the "good," "pure" child; Steinlen's and Manet's cats with their insouciance, all of these have an elegant sense of wit and humor.

It is within the context forged by the dual

movements of *Japonisme* and the rise of artistic printmaking that Henri Rivière was able to create his own artwork. Japanese art offered Rivière a source from which to draw inspiration, and the renaissance in printmaking provided him with a medium that suited his talents and outlook. From the Japanese style he incorporated a flat sense of space, broad application of color, and a varying perspective, yet he retained his individuality as an artist and cannot be considered as an imitator. He was not alone in applying these methods, as most of his contemporaries did the same. In fact, Rivière and Lautrec were born in the same year, and Auriol, Bonnard, Denis, Ibels, Lunois, Munch, Signac, Steinlen, Roussel, and Vuillard were all born within several years of Rivière. These artists were the second generation to break with tradition, following the lead begun by the artists born in the 1830s such as Manet, Degas, Whistler, and Pissarro. The artists of this second generation became even more daring and experimental in their approach to art, breaking more completely with tradition than did their predecessors, expanding the path initiated by them. Many became printmakers primarily, as did Rivière, and many illustrated books, as did Rivière, thereby creating an entirely new area of artistic expression, the *livre d'artiste*. These artists helped to create an environment in which art can exist on many levels and in many forms.

Of all the artists who did master graphic techniques in the period 1890-1910, it is Rivière who stands foremost as a landscapist. In his art, the seashore, waves, cliffs, rocks, and trees predominate. Man and his effects form a secondary, but complementary, part of his pictures. When people are portrayed, it is the life of the group, not the individual, which is shown: the everyday life of villagers washing laundry, attending a funeral, returning home from the fields or preparing to set sail for the day's catch of fish; these are the scenes Rivière shows us. Nature always dominates in his scenes, whether it be a view of a Breton bay with a small sailboat being swept along by the wind, or young boys climbing over massive rocks, their small forms overshadowed by the hugeness of the land. More often than not, it is Nature herself which Rivière strove to reveal: waves crashing on rocks, a snowstorm blanketing a village, sunrise, sunset, moonrise, a rainbow over a field, the changing seasons. It is not a harsh, terrifying Nature he paints, but rather, a peaceful, benevolent one, contemplative and harmonious. These images occur over and over again in all of his graphic series, *Le Beau Pays de Bretagne, Au Vent de Noroit, Les Aspects de la Nature, La Féerie des Heures*. Even in his series of Paris, tellingly titled *Parisian Landscapes*, Rivière shows the city in landscape terms. His broad horizons and vistas are seen from vantage points high enough atop the Butte Montmartre or Notre Dame to show panoramic views, while scenes taken at a low angle, the edge of the Seine, show a wide, low horizon. While

Lautrec excelled at portraying the demimonde and theatrical worlds, Bonnard concentrated on the lively activities of Parisians, Vuillard revealed Parisian interiors, Lunois created scenes of the exotic and far-away, and Redon opened the world of mystery and imagination, it was Rivière who concentrated on the land and sea, on the countryside and its changing attributes.

The majority of Rivière's work and nearly all of his graphic oeuvre was done in the 1890s and early 1900s, yet he continued to paint until his death in 1951. He seemed not to care that he was not represented by any gallery, or that his work was rarely publicly exhibited; he seems to have been content existing outside the circles and movements which flourished around him after the First World War. But until the early years of the twentieth century, Rivière was an active participant in the Parisian art world, enjoyed popular and critical success, and was very much a part of the avante-garde printmaking.

From his earliest years Rivière had the desire to become an artist, and although faced with parental discouragement, little money, and very brief training, he nevertheless pursued his goal with determination and enthusiasm, qualities which would characterize him throughout his life. Rivière pursued his object regardless of outside influences or pressures. During the course of his career, his art teacher, his printer, his patron, and his publisher all died in the midst of working with Rivière, yet he persistently continued to work on his own, in his own fashion, productively and creatively, despite these dramatic setbacks. Rivière was concerned with the process of art. He diligently taught himself the arts of woodcutting, photography, and ceramics. He habitually learned new skills by doing them, receiving little or no instruction from anyone else. He became an artist despite his lack of training; he became a connoisseur and collector without the advantages of great wealth, a fine education, or family tradition. His sensibilities and sensitivities were such that he was able to lead a life of creativity and productivity, integrity and achievement, fulfilling all that he undertook.

Beginnings
1864-1881

BENJAMIN JEAN PIERRE HENRI RIVIÈRE was born on 11 May 1864 in Paris at 135 rue de Montmartre. His father, Prosper Rivière, was a successful embroidery merchant who had been in Paris for some years after a boyhood spent in the Pyrénées. His mother, Henriette Thérèse Leroux Rivière, was a Parisienne from a petit bourgeois family. Henri was the couple's first child; a second son, Jules, was born fifteen months later. Henri and Jules began their schooling at the ages of five and four, but this enrollment was shortly interrupted by the outbreak of the Franco-Prussian War in 1870. Prosper Rivière deemed it best for the family to leave Paris. He closed his embroidery business, stored the materials, and took the family to the place of his birth, Aix-les-Thermes, in the Pyrénées. There were Rivière relatives there, including an uncle, the notary of the town, who was very fond of the children and with whom the family stayed.

Henri and Jules were pleased with their new surroundings, the mountains, forests, and rivers, so unlike what they had been accustomed to in Paris, and there they remained throughout the war. It was during this period of his life that Rivière developed his love of nature, which was to become the predominant theme in his art.

Shortly after the end of the war, Henri returned to Paris with his parents while his brother remained at Aix in order to finish his education under the care of their uncle. It was Jules, who showed abilities in mathematics, whom the family thought had a promising future and his education was overseen with greater care than that of Henri. While the brothers saw one another periodically, they were to be separated for the next nine years, until 1880.

Henriette Therese Leroux Rivière

Henri Rivière at six months

Prosper Rivière

Rivière was enrolled in a boarding school outside of Paris where he was unhappy and lonely. Rivière's father developed the first signs of an illness from which he ultimately died in 1873. His mother attempted to keep the embroidery business going, but life became difficult for Rivière. The family moved to a cheaper apartment and, soon thereafter, moved again. Henri was enrolled in a local day school where he became friendly with another local boy, Paul Signac, the son of a local harnessmaker. They maintained their friendship, and would soon be studying art together.

In 1875 Rivière's mother was married again, to Léon Fruger, a local government official whom Rivière liked very much. Their circumstances improved, and Rivière began attending a local day school, the Colbert Academy. He excelled in two subjects: reading and painting. He read voraciously, especially Hugo and Verne, and he zealously awaited the weekly installments of their stories in the illustrated journals. By this time, Rivière had his own set of paints, and he spent a great deal of time painting, mostly copying pictures by Doré or Vièrge from the pages of the weekly magazines. On Sundays he went up to the Butte Montmartre to paint, or to the Louvre or the Luxembourg museums, "where I spent long hours in admiration before the pictures, whose entire beauty I was far from understanding but which plunged me into delight."

In 1879 there appeared a weekly magazine which was unlike any other of the time: *La Vie*

Moderne. What made it so extraordinary were its illustrations, which were not black-and-white wood engravings like the other journals, but were color *Gillotypes,*—color photoengravings. Charles Gillot had invented the process to faithfully reproduce drawings and sketches. It involved making color separations for each color to be printed. It required technical mastery of both photography and engraving, as the separations were prepared by a skilled engraver and the plates were made by a photographer. Interestingly enough, this process, which altered the course of color printing, was invented by an ardent collector of Japanese prints, who was perhaps influenced by them in his invention. In *La Vie Moderne* the texts of Daudet, Flaubert, de Goncourt, Zola, and many others were illustrated by the leading artists of the day. For Rivière, the magazine was a feast, and it confirmed his desire to draw and paint. He saw in its pages for the first time the works of Monet, Renoir, Manet, Sisley, and Pissarro, all reproduced in color. That the color on the pages of *La Vie Moderne* so impressed Rivière is an early indication of just how important color would later be in his own work. But in the 1870s and early 1880s, color in prints was limited to the pages of magazines and advertisements; it had not found a place in original printmaking.

Although Rivière desired to become an artist, his mother had a different future planned for him. She secured a job for him in the firm of a feather merchant. The job lasted one week. Bored and frustrated, Rivière picked up his materials and went to the Butte to paint, but he was quickly found out. His mother, who was very vexed by her son's behavior, told his stepfather, who in turn told a friend of the situation. The friend was Père Bin, the "Mayor of Montmartre," an old academic painter and art teacher. Bin asked to see Rivière's work, and upon viewing it, asked to have Rivière sent to him "starting tomorrow." Rivière was admitted to Bin's studio and began the only formal art training he ever received. Another of Bin's pupils was Rivière's friend Paul Signac, and while they did not attend the same classes, they often worked together. Unfortunately, after about a year and a half, Père Bin died, leaving Rivière on his own.

During the time Rivière was in art school, his brother Jules returned to Paris and entered the Collège Rollin. By the end of the academic year, Jules had passed his university entrance exams, for which he received a gift of 500 francs from his uncle's estate. With the money, Jules and Henri decided to take a vacation. Signac had recommended a spot in Brittany, St. Briac, and upon this suggestion the brothers set out. It was Rivière's introduction to the area he was to visit, live in, and paint for many years to come.

Throughout the summer of 1881, Rivière did much watercolor painting in the countryside. One day, returning home in the late afternoon, he chanced to meet Renoir. "We saw, sitting on his campstool, a painter, who had in front of him a peasant woman, looking after a cow. I watched him discreetly at some distance and I was quickly convinced on looking at his painting that it was Renoir who was before us. With the assurance of youth, I ventured near him, and raising my hat to him said:

'Good day Monsieur Renoir.'

'Do you know me then young man?'

'No, monsieur, I recognized you by your painting.'

Henri Rivière at eighteen years

'Oh, how kind this young expert is,' said Renoir as he noticed my box of colors:

'But I think you must be a colleague?'

And I was obliged to show him my study, which he was kind enough not to find too inept.''

Summer over, the brothers returned to Paris, and Henri was faced with a critical decision: his mother gave him the choice of entering a business or going out on his own as an artist. Rivière chose the latter. He found a small attic room in Montmartre, was given some furniture and a small amount of money by his parents, and so set himself up as an artist.

Rivière had made friends with several artists and writers, including Eugène Torquet, who later won prizes as a writer, Charles Torquet, his brother, Maurice Sallinger, the Bonnet brothers, and Signac. They formed a club, ''The Epileptic, Baudelarian, and Anti-Philistine Red Herrings,'' where they discussed art, literature, and poetry.

Of this period, Rivière said: ''I spent my days drawing and painting, seeing my little store of money gradually disappearing, without hope of renewing it. Fortunately, an important change was going to allow me to provide more for my maintenance and let me know about a whole world of which I knew nothing.''

At eighteen, Rivière was to be introduced to Rudolphe Salis and his cabaret, the Chat Noir. This environment was to open Rivière's artistic world.

Chat Noir
1881-1896

RUDOLPHE SALIS, a one-time painter and entertainer, decided to open a cabaret in Montmartre to attract artists, poets, and musicians. It was his idea to have artists decorate the cabaret and have the employees dress sardonically as academic painters. The cabaret would be a place for artists to sing, dance, and perform their works unhindered. Among the early contributors were Steinlen, Willette, Goudeau, Caran d'Ache, and Grasset. It was opened in November 1881, and was called the Chat Noir. "The place was pleasant: a stained-glass front, a big shop sign cut out in sheet metal after a design of Willette, a black cat on a silver crescent moon, with walls of green, a big country fireplace whose mantel was adorned with copper and rustic pottery. Above the chest where Madame Salis was enthroned, a sun with golden rays with a cat's head in the center sculpted by Fremiet, chandeliers of wrought iron, designed by Grasset, chairs, oak tables, a completely harmonious decor unique in Paris of that time." And upon the walls were displayed the drawings of his friends.

The Chat Noir was unique in Montmartre and in all of Paris. Its performers made fun of the social and political mores of the time. The cabaret's music and art were integrated into its daily operation and allowed the performers and customers to exchange and share these experiences. Since the cabaret emphasized this kind of milieu, many of the customers were from the upper social and literate levels. The cabaret offered them an opportunity to "let off steam" in a legitimate manner in an otherwise conservative social class.

The Chat Noir quickly became a famous and popular spot, and Salis embarked upon the publication of a journal to feature the poems, thoughts, articles, and artwork of the habitues. Named after the cabaret, the first issue of *Chat Noir* appeared on 14 January 1882. Emile Goudeau was the editor in chief, assisted by Edmond Deschaumes; Henri Pille created the masthead, a black cat in front of the windmills of Montmartre.

Many of the artistic creations at the Chat Noir, including the design and layout of its journal, were affected by the Japanese influence in Paris at the time. A number of artists and writers employed there had already demonstrated their interest in Japonisme. Now they were able to incorporate it into their artistic endeavors at the cabaret.

One day, Rivière was taken to the cabaret by Signac and Torquet; he soon became a frequent visitor. His literary and artistic talents were soon put to use, as he was offered the job of assistant secretary of the journal, replacing Deschaumes who had other work to do. The job consisted of editing all the material to be published in the journal. Rivière was overjoyed, for not only did he obtain a job, but it was one which utilized his interests and talents and permitted him to associate with fellow artists. Besides his salary, he received his lunch and dinner at the cabaret. This position put Rivière in the center of the artistic and literary world of Montmartre, the artistic center of Paris. It was also at this time that Rivière was introduced to etching, probably by Grasset or Caran d'Ache, both of whom frequented the Chat Noir. Rivière made four etchings from his summer sketches of Brittany, and printed them in blue in very small editions of five to ten. He sold very few, and gave most of them to friends. Between 1881 and 1885, Rivière completed ten etchings. He then abandoned the medium and didn't use it again until 1906.

Program for the Theatre Libre, *lithograph, 1890, 16x20 cm.*

Paul Signac

George Auriol

Henry Somm

Adolphe Willette

Salis liked and was protective of Rivière, who was the youngest participant at the Chat Noir. Rivière worked daily with Willette, Steinlen, Grasset, Somm, Pille, and Caran d'Ache, and he soon met George Auriol, the designer of stage sets, books, and programs, with whom he began a long friendship. They worked together on many projects, and it was Auriol who later designed Rivière's cachets which he used to sign his prints.

By 1885 the Chat Noir had become well known and busy, and expansion was necessary. Salis wanted to enlarge it, add new decorations and expand the stage presentations. A new site was found, the former studio of the painter Alfred Stevens on the rue Victor Massé, and renovation was begun immediately. Painters, sculptors, masons, carpenters, paperhangers all set to work, and within four or five months the Hotel de Stevens was transformed into the new Cabaret au Chat Noir. Henry Somm built a puppet theater and Jules Jouy sang and played the piano to accompany the plays.

There is some question how the shadow theater was started at the new Chat Noir. Rivière suggested that he was not responsible for the original idea. His friend Auriol, however, indicated that it all started as a joke on Jules Jouy. While Jouy was performing on stage one evening, the stage lights were darkened, much to Jouy's surprise. A spotlight was put on the puppet stage, shining against a white screen, and figures were seen to move across the screen. The audience response was positive, with lively applause.

Rivière had the idea of formalizing the program and attempting to tell a story (or supply background for a story being recited on stage) with the use of the screen and silhouettes. On a platform behind the stage, cut-out figures were placed, illuminated from behind, and moved across the stage. Their shadows were projected onto a screen, and the *Shadow Theatre* was born. Rivière had the idea of making the stage larger and producing spectacular shadow plays with themes taken from history, fairy tales, the Bible, and Greek classics. He proposed this plan to Salis, who was enthusiastic and asked Rivière to become the new stage director. The new stage was built, a huge one, two stories in height and the width of the entire building. By fall of 1886 the stage was completed and the first major production was launched, *L'Epopée* by Caran d'Ache. It was a great success. From then on, Rivière supervised all the shadow plays, creating several himself. In the eleven years of its existence, forty-three shadow plays were produced at the Chat Noir.

Rivière and his colleagues working on a shadow theater production. Rivière is standing in the foreground. (From a drawing by Georges Redon in 1893.)

The first images at the Chat Noir were cut out of zinc and the shadows simply shown on a screen through the use of back lighting. After the first few presentations, Rivière improved it by creating perspective with his zinc cutouts. Later, Rivière introduced the use of colored lighting and colored paper in the production, and the audience's response to these innovations was overwhelming. Skies and water could be illuminated in shades of blue and green; the landscapes could feature browns, reds, and yellows. And the images of people could be seen to pass across the screen, moving up and down to simulate the buffeting of waves or the contours of the land.

But Rivière was not finished innovating for the shadow theater. In 1890, with his production of "La Marche à L'Etoile," Rivière introduced moving colored lights to create such effects as the changes of day into night, of clouds moving across the horizon, the colors of an approaching storm, of moonlight and sunlight illuminating the land or water. He produced a picture where time and distance could be compressed into moments and where landscapes, oceans, and mountains could be seen fleeting by. Many pieces of colored glass, enameled and baked by Rivière himself, were hung on wires and placed on runners across the stage. Certain combinations of the colored glass were lit by an oxhydrogenic apparatus as they were pulled along the runners. For some performances, Rivière and his colleagues operated 150 pieces of glass.

In 1888 Rivière, by then a well-known figure in Montmartre, was asked to participate in an exhibition of the works of the Chat Noir artists to be held at the Pavillion de la Ville de Paris, the city hall. Among the other artists who exhibited were Caran d'Ache, Grasset, Robida, Rops, Steinlen, Somme, and Willette. Rivière exhibited etchings, watercolors, and theater designs; it was his first public showing.

At this time Rivière met Eugenie Estelle Ley, the twenty-four-year-old daughter of a government finance official. They became lovers and it was the beginning of the intimate relationship that lasted a lifetime. Eugenie helped to organize Rivière's personal affairs so that he could spend his time on his art, and by the following year, they decided to live together. In describing Eugenie, Rivière wrote: "I had met in 1888 the lady who was my dear companion for more than half a century; we were two young people . . . who loved each other with a tender mutual trust, which has never been disappointed. She always smoothed away from my path the material preoccupations of life to let me devote myself completely to my work."

Unlike many of his friends and co-workers, Rivière was neither interested nor involved in the available excesses of Montmartre life. While he smoked a great deal, he drank rarely, was very devoted to Eugenie, and hardly at all participated in the ever-present parties and artist's get-togethers. Along with his daily Chat Noir responsibilities, Rivière devoted his time and effort to his personal artistic endeavors.

In 1888 Sigfried Bing, an Oriental art dealer, began publication of *Le Japon Artistique,* a journal devoted to the study and presentation of Japanese art and artifacts. Interest in Japanese art had been steadily increasing since it began to be imported to Paris in the 1860s. By the 1880s Japanese art was having a tremendous influence on Western artists. Rivière, like most of the artists of the period had responded to the Japanese style. With the appearance of *Le Japon Artistique* his interest was greatly aroused. He began to collect examples of Japanese arts and crafts and to learn about their history and manufacture. Most importantly, he began to teach himself to make woodblock prints in the Japanese manner. Collecting and studying Oriental art was to become a lifelong hobby. Making woodblock prints was to be a creative challenge which absorbed his energies for the next five years.

Friends of the Chat Noir. Standing (far right): Rivière. Sitting (Rivière's hand on head): Paul Signac.

"Du Viaduc d'Auteuil," woodcut, 4 colors, proof
for 36 Views of the Eiffel Tower, *edition of 3,*
1891, 17x20 cm.

Rivière was so taken with the Japanese woodblock technique that, with characteristic determination and enthusiasm, he made his own cutting tools, learned to cut blocks by trial and error, mixed all of his own inks and did all of his own printing. He was able to buy antique Japanese paper on which to print the blocks. He accomplished all of this in less than a year. It was not until many years later, while he was showing his friend Tadamasa Hayashi his woodblock technique, that Hayashi marveled at the work and told Rivière that his tools, cutting, ink, and printing techniques were exactly like those used by Japanese artists 200 years earlier.

At the time of Rivière's initial interest in woodcuts, Paris was preparing for a large international exhibition to be held in 1890, largely devoted to technical and industrial achievements. One technical marvel under construction was an iron tower designed by Alexandre Eiffel. Rivière began sketching the tower as it underwent construction and turned some sketches into his first woodblock prints. He made two woodblocks and found the cutting and printing to be difficult; he set aside the project, which ultimately was published in 1902 as *Les Trente-Six Vues de la Tour Eiffel,* with the views printed in lithography rather than woodcut.

Rivière undertook another woodblock project, a series of Breton landscapes. He was invited to exhibit them at the Société de Peintre-Graveurs exhibition held at the Durand-Ruel

"Clairs de Lune," announcement for the book
of poems, music, and lithographs of the same
title, lithograph, 6 colors, 1896, 29x78 cm.

Gallery, and he "continued with desperate eagerness to increase their number. To manage in time for the exhibition, I had only been able to print ten examples instead of twenty per plate . . . I made the colors myself, ground them and mixed them . . . I printed my plates by hand with twenty examples of each. The woodcuts shown represented, with six to ten colors per plate, nearly 250 printings. I have never been able, as I have been taken up with other work, to finish the series of *Breton Landscapes*. . . ." Despite this, Rivière seemed to favor the woodcut over any other graphic process, and described the process: "If the printing is difficult, at least it is absorbing; it takes you back to your artistic craft, to the pleasure of matching tones and colors. To engrave or etch is amusing; it is a drawing that you make by a process other than the pencil or pen, that's all! But to cut with your knife, against wood grain, the contours of a lined plank is not attractive, it is a purely manual craft where the mind scarcely intervenes . . . how many thousands of insipid gouges must you make only to bring into relief the parts to be printed!"

Rivière worked intensely on his woodcuts, creating most of them between 1890 and 1894. His were some of the finest woodcuts of the period. Rivière's use of carved line detail was comparable to the Hokusai and Hiroshige wood carvers, and his use of extensive color (sometimes up to twelve colors in an image) far surpassed that of any other artist working with woodblocks. His exacting registration was never even attempted by his fellow artists.

But most important was his blending of the Brittany landscape—a Western artist's view of nature—with the Japanese style of perspective, high horizons and flat color. This combination created a picture that the critic Sarradin said was the "quintessence of nature." With near mathematical perfection, Rivière produced an image of delicacy, correctness, and accuracy of tone achieved through a simple, almost primitive means. Thus, the image remains fresh and the colors radiant even today.

During 1889 Rivière produced five plays at the Théâtre d'Ombres, continued to edit the *Chat Noir* journal, worked on his woodblocks, and set up housekeeping with Eugenie. In the summer, he and Eugenie decided to go to Brittany and spend their time in St. Briac. Rivière did a great deal of sketching and painting and made preliminary drawings for his woodblock series *Paysages Bretons*, which would ultimately include forty images, the first nineteen of which were completed by 1890 and shown at the Durand-Ruel exhibit. Thus began a pattern of sketching summers in Brittany, followed by winters in Paris where the sketches were turned into printed editions.

In the autumn of 1887 Andre Antoine, whom Rivière had known at the Chat Noir, founded his own theatre, the Théâtre Libre, an avant-garde theatre featuring the works of Ibsen, Strindberg, Checkhov, and others. Antoine wanted to have his

"Le Pont des Saint-Pères et le Louvre,"
lithograph, 12 colors, from Paysages Parisiens
series, no. 6, 1900, 52.5x82 cm.

theatre programs prepared by artists, and in 1890 Rivière was asked to create one. He accepted the commission, joining the ranks of Ibels, Signac, Lautrec, Willette, and Auriol. He prepared a Parisian scene with a strong Japanese feeling to it, both in its diptych image and its colors of gray, pink, and white. The piece was to be lithographed, a medium until now unknown to Rivière. Antoine introduced Rivière to Eugene Verneau, a commercial lithographic printer who was just beginning to become interested in the printing of fine art and who was interested in having artists work directly with his printers. Verneau had already printed all of Antoine's programs since 1888, including Signac's *Cercle Chromatique de Charles Henry,* one of the earliest examples of the full use of color in printmaking. As technical innovations made the printing of color lithographs easier, artists began to be interested in exploring the use of color in their work. Printmaking had been predominantly a black-and-white medium, and color was slow to find acceptance by print connoisseurs. These theater programs served as a bridge between commercial color printing and original artistic printmaking. Antoine's idea was a catalyst: it gave artists an immediate outlet for their work and opened the way for them to begin to use color on their own. The programs were commercial in the sense that they served as advertisements, but they afforded the artists their first contact with color printmaking, and color

printmaking became the preferred medium of the 1890s.

Rivière found lithography to his liking, and he began to spend a great deal of time at Verneau's studio. He carried his woodblock printing experiences into lithography. Not only did he reproduce images of the Brittany landscape but he continued to use many of the Japanese techniques he had mastered. In his first lithographs, we see use of layered perspective, the high horizon lines, large objects in the foreground, flat color, and partial images cut off by the picture's edge. As Rivière continued his lithographic work, these features developed in maturity and became a unique part of his style. Rivière also experimented with the use of color in lithography. While his friend Signac might have been one of the first to use color in lithography, it was Rivière who worked with larger numbers of colors in an image, who would overlay them in printing, and who would mix the colors with varnish to give them different textures and hues. In addition, it was Rivière who produced many color editions in large numbers before any of his colleagues. For these reasons, many consider Rivière the "father of color lithography."

The relationship between Rivière and Verneau grew into a strong friendship, and their collaboration produced some of the most beautiful color lithographs of the period. Rivière describes Verneau and his workshop with affection: "He was a good-hearted man, who was very interested in

Announcement for the series Au Vent de Noroit
(including other previously published series),
lithograph, 8 colors, 1906, 23x60 cm.

artists. He was a fairly stout fellow, jovial and amusing . . . he was well liked by all those who approached him. His little printing works in the rue de la Folie Mericourt, where the workers were paternally treated like children of the house, prospered rapidly. . . . It was really a good house, where each one did his work by becoming interested in it, which seems to me to have, unhappily, become rare enough today."

For his second lithographic effort Rivière created another program for Antoine. During the next few years he continued to experiment at the Verneau studio. In 1893 he was asked to contribute a picture to the new quarterly art album *L'Estampe Originale,* published under the direction of Andre Marty in collaboration with Roger Marx. *L'Estampe Originale* was to consist of quarterly albums of ten prints in all graphic media, and was representative of the new directions printmaking was taking. By 1895, when its publication ceased, *L'Estampe Originale* had presented ninety-five prints (by seventy-four artists), twenty-eight of

which were color lithographs. Rivière's contribution was *La Vague,* a color lithograph of a wave in the Japanese style.

In 1895 Rivière and Eugenie were married. He was continuing his watercolors in the Japanese style and working on his woodcuts, although at a slower pace. He had completed five in 1892, and only one each in 1893 and 1894. He would not return to the woodblock technique until 1913. Articles on Rivière began to appear, the first in 1893 by Louis Moran, published in the journal *L'Artiste.* It was very complimentary to the artist and his work. Other articles were published, including an article in an 1896 issue of the important English journal *The Studio.*

By 1895 the Chat Noir had begun to decline, the journal ceased publication, and in 1896 the shadow theater ended with the death of Salis. An important era was over, not only for Rivière but for many artists and writers who began their careers at the Chat Noir. It had been a focal point, a place where ideas and theories were shared, and it was the inspiration for the journal which in turn inspired such later publications as *Le Rire, Le Mirliton, Cocorico, La Plume,* and others.

Another phase of Rivière's life had come to an end. The next phase had already started, however, with his deep involvement in lithography. At the same time, Rivière had been gaining a considerable reputation in Paris as one of the foremost artists. The next few years were to see him reach his peak in Parisian artistic circles.

Color Lithography and Japonisme
1896-1902

RIVIERE continued working on various other projects after the closing of the Chat Noir. He was asked to illustrate several books based on the shadow theatre, converting his *tableaux* into color lithographs. Four books were published: *La Marche à l'Etoile, L'Enfant Prodigue, Claires de Lune,* and *Le Juif Errant.* During the summer of 1896 Rivière and his wife moved into their newly completed summer home in Brittany, at Loguivy, which they named *Landiris.* The choice of the name was significant, for Rivière loved irises and they appeared in his cachets, his artworks, and his surroundings throughout his life. The location of the house was especially selected by Rivière, on a "high cliff going down to the sea in several plunges, covered with pines, carpeted with heather and gorse among grey rocks. . . . You could believe yourself at the end of the world there, in still virgin countryside, where the noise of the winds and the sea, the cries of birds, a sail beating as it changed tack, the call of a sailor, were the only sounds which enlivened the harmonious landscape, which changed in itself and its colors according to the effects and the hours. . . ." This description could apply to any number of Rivière's lithographs of Brittany, and he was to paint many pictures of the surrounding countryside from his doorstep each summer for over seventeen years.

During this period, he and Mme. Rivière moved from relatively small quarters in Montmartre to a larger apartment on the top floor of a building on the Boulevard de Clichy overlooking much of the city. Rivière now had room to house his ever-expanding collection of Oriental art and examples of his own work. And he now had a studio of his own.

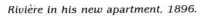
Rivière in his new apartment, 1896.

Rivière, in front of his summer home, Landiris, c. 1896.

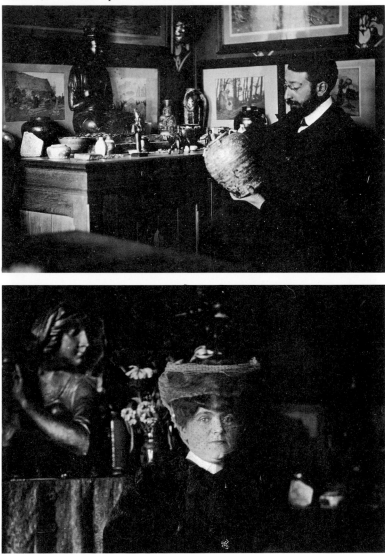
Madame Rivière, 1896

In 1896 Rivière published his first major lithograph edition. At the time he championed the idea that prints should be large in size, be issued in large editions, and be sold for relatively inexpensive prices. Such ideas had gained some popularity, and Charles Verneau had become interested in printing these works, called *l'estampe murale.* They were used to decorate homes, schools, shops, restaurants, and the like, and several artists including Grasset, Steinlen, and Raffaelli had worked with Verneau in printing such works.

These large prints were reflective of the major change in attitude towards printmaking: serious artists could produce handsome, decorative works for use by the public in order to improve the overall visual environment. Because they were cheap no longer meant prints had to be ugly or vulgar. Fine artists could create fine prints in large editions and no longer suffer the social stigma formerly attached to such activity. To Rivière, with his lack of pretensions and forthright, honest nature, this idea was especially appealing.

Rivière's first major edition was therefore an "interior wall print," and was published by one of the leading publishers of the day, Librairie Larousse. *L'Hiver* was issued in an edition of 1000. Both the size of the edition and the size of the print, 54.5 x 83cm., broke dramatically with tradition, and it was an instant success. The first print was a depiction of winter, and perhaps he intended to do a series of the four seasons. But he

Rivière in his studio, c. 1896.

21

"L'Hiver" (Image pour l'ecole no. 1), lithograph,
12 colors, edition of 1,000, 1896, 54.5x83 cm.

and Eugene Verneau then decided to collaborate instead on a series of large format, large edition lithographs. The set of sixteen images under the general title *Les Aspects de la Nature* was begun. Six images appeared in 1897, six in 1898, and the remaining four in 1899.

Rivière's involvement with color lithography was part of the general movement towards freer expression and unlimited scope and originality in the graphic arts. Color lithography had moved away from the domain of the commercial printers who had used the medium for advertising and illustrating, and into the camp of the artists. Because lithography was best suited of all the graphic methods to color printing, artists readily took to it and it became the striking new medium of the 1890s. And what a bold move it was, for even in 1897 the annual Salon of the Society of French Artists forbade the exhibition of color prints. The old guard Academicians argued against color in prints as untraditional. Hadn't the masterpieces of Durer, Rembrandt and Goya been created in black and white, they reasoned? But the innovative artists championed the use of color: it was modern, expressive, bold, and attractive. The Japanese had shown what could be accomplished with color. Manet had experimented with it in his *Polichinelle* of 1874 and Cheret developed the color poster. But during the 1870s and 1880s there was no real movement towards color. Yet by the 1890s color was the major force on the printmaking

"Le Crépuscule," lithograph, from Les Aspects de la Nature, *no. 8, 1898, 54.5x83 cm.*

"Le Fleuve," lithograph, from Les Aspects de la Nature, *no. 6, 1897, 54.5x83 cm.*

"De l'île des Cygnes," lithograph, 5 colors,
Les Trente-Six Vues de la Tour Eiffel, *no. 24,*
1888-1902, 17x20 cm.

"L'Institute et la Cité," lithograph, from
Paysages Parisiens, no. 4, 1900, 52.5x82 cm.

horizon, and in 1899 the Salon finally accepted color prints.

By 1898 Rivière was sufficiently respected to be included in Andre Mellerio's pioneering work on color lithography *La Lithographie en Couleurs.* Mellerio's work was the first major critical work on color in lithography and the artists who best used it. It is in fact one of the first French *libres d'artiste* with its color lithographic frontispiece and covers by Bonnard. Rivière is the eighth artist Mellerio discusses, after Lautrec, Bonnard, Ibels, Vuillard, Denis, Roussel, and Lunois. Thirty-two artists follow Rivière, including Steinlen and Signac. Mellerio perceptively analyzes Rivière's work: "M. Henri Rivière has produced a series of 'decorative prints,' justly named. Their size, the intention of attaching them to walls and framing them for ornamentation of our interiors, makes them something other than a collector's item destined for the portfolio. What is most striking about M. Rivière's work is the combination of a very real feeling for nature with a harmonic sense of the organization of line and color. From this comes a mixed impression reminding us, when we add the use of flat tones, of the flavor of Japanese prints, but without any suggestion of a plagiaristic copy. M. Rivière's colors, because of their more gentle scale, belong to a Western eye. He is less preoccupied with pure arabesque, and his urge to simplification never gives way to the deformations of fantasy. It should be recognized that the artist always stresses the most strikingly decorative

"Quai d'Austerlitz," lithograph, from Paysages
Parisiens, no. 3, 1900 52.5x82 cm.

Madame Epstein-Langweil, c. 1900

*Rivière and his brother Jules examining
Oriental artifacts, c. 1900.*

parts of the landscape, at the same time retaining all of its poetry. . . .''

Rivière avidly continued adding to his Oriental art collection. Most of his friends were like-minded connoisseurs and collectors, among them Auriol, Bing, the Dauphin family of poets and musicians, Pierre Moreau, and Odon Guneau de Mussy, an elegant dilettante. In 1897 Rivière was taken by de Mussy to a shop he did not know, a small place on the Boulevard des Italiens owned by Mme. Florine Epstein-Langweil. Rivière was fascinated by what he saw there: ancient jade, rock crystals, precious stones, ancient pottery. He was intrigued by Mme. Langweil and her daughter Berthe, and they became close friends. Florine Epstein was born in Alsace in 1861 and came to Paris in 1882. She was married to Charles Langweil in 1884; their daughter Berthe was born in 1886. Her husband left her in 1893, so Mme. Langweil took over his antique shop, familiarized herself with Oriental art, and began to specialize in Japanese works. She soon developed a reputation for carrying fine pieces and unique examples at reasonable prices. Her honesty and friendly nature attracted many collectors. Her shop was one of several Rivière and other Japanophiles frequented in Paris. Rivière recalled visiting Bing's shop with his friend George Auriol:

"George Auriol and I had a great admiration for Japanese art, not very well known until then in France. Guneau de Mussy shared this admiration and it was he who introduced us to

Siegfried Bing—in his premises in the rue de Provence. They let us leaf through albums and prints for long afternoons of our initiation by ourselves: they well knew that we were not buyers but that we were forming new skills. We also gazed curiously at the cabinets of lacquers, pottery, and ancient bronzes, of scabbards of rich materials, but we were content to look at all these precious things without being able to touch them. . . . It is true that our preference at that time was for prints above all, which looked so new to us Europeans. Obviously, it was necessary that our Western eyes, used to relief, to the play of light and shadow, to the volume of people and things, be gradually involved in the way of seeing things that the artists of the Far East had. We discovered a new way of expressing ourselves and that didn't happen without some difficulty or restrictions. . . . The exotic perfume of these works charmed us and also amused us. . . . And it was a great pleasure to discover one after the other, first of all the Primitives, like Moronobu, with their prints in black, then in two tones, black and pink; then in three, black, pink, and green (Kiyonobu, Masamobu); and there were the polychrome printings (four, six, or eight colors), the daring simplifications of Korin, the bold Haronobu, the attractive Koryusai, the elegant Kiyonaga, the gracious Utamaro, Sharaku, Shunso, Toyokuni, and so many others. . . . And we reached the creator of tireless invention, this 'old man mad about drawing' as he called himself, Hokusai. . . . For more than a hundred years, he transfixed on paper tragic or elegiac scenes. . . . Finally, there was the landscapist Hiroshige. . . . who showed us the real shape of his beautiful country in all weathers. . . ."

Through this network of connoisseurs, Rivière also met Marcel Bing, son of Siegfried, and Degas. On Fridays, Rivière would meet with his friends and fellow collectors to show, share, and discuss their finds. A "secret" society was formed, *Le Cenacle*, of which Rivière was vice-president. They were following in a tradition of "secret" art societies, including the *Société du Jing-Iar*, the first group devoted to the study of Japanese art, formed in the 1860s. *Le Cenacle* occasionally met at Degas's house on the rue Victor Massé, and when Degas moved to the Boulevard de Clichy close to Rivière's apartment, the two met often and continued to do so until Degas's death in 1917. Rivière's friendship with Degas would enable him to compile a lavish book about Degas's drawings in 1922.

Another of Rivière's contacts in the Oriental art world was Tadamasa Hayashi, who became a close friend and patron. Hayashi, born in 1851, studied at Tokyo Imperial University, became fluent in French and was hired as an interpreter to the company which organized Japan's participation in the Paris Universal Exhibition of 1878. After the close of the exhibition, Hayashi remained in Paris, continuing to work for the company. In 1884 he and another employee left their work in order to set up shop as art dealers. Hayashi ended the partnership in 1889 and began independent activities. Hayashi imported thousands of *ukiyo-e* prints and helped to form the major collections built by Vever, Haviland, de Gocourt, and others. In 1900 Hayashi was appointed by the Japanese government to serve as the Commissioner General of the International Exhibition. He organized the

Tadamasa Hayashi.

Japanese pavilion, where spectators could view ancient Japanese art, theatrical performances, and the like. Hayashi was also a collector of French art—one of the first Japanese to do so—and he had in his collection works by Corot, Degas, and Rivière. He asked Rivière to paint a set of murals to decorate his Tokyo home. Rivière suggested four panels, each portraying a season, each covering a whole wall. Rivière estimated it would take two years to complete the project, and gave a relatively low figure as his fee. Hayashi, surprised at the modest cost, offered Rivière the choice of anything in his shop, which he was preparing to close, as compensation. Thus Rivière was able to add to his collection many rare and unusual pieces. Hayashi closed the business in 1901, leaving the remaining stock in Bing's care for an upcoming auction, a monumental sale of nearly 1,800 works which was held in June 1902. Hayashi left Paris in 1905 and returned to Japan, where he suddenly became ill and died. Hayashi and Bing had dominated the trend in *ukiyo-e* prints and were responsible for many artists acquiring large collections, including Monet, Van Gogh, Rivière, and others. Hayashi provided a link between Japan and France, and his genuine interest brought to France an artform which was underappreciated in Japan.

Rivière continued to work in color lithography, and began a new series, *Le Beau Pays de Bretagne.* He also had the idea of making a calendar each year utilizing one of the images of the series as its central image. These calendars

"Morgat," watercolor, 1905, 26x41 cm.

were not only useful and decorative, they served as advertising for the series itself and were very successful. Another series was begun, *Paysages Parisiens*, a set of eight views of the city, once again large in format and edition. During 1901-02 Rivière published the series *La Féerie des Heures*, a set of sixteen lithographs strongly influenced by Japanese works. Rivière completed another important project, one which had occupied his time on and off since 1888: recording the building of the Eiffel Tower. He had completed his sketches in the 1890s, and had made two of the images into woodcuts, but had abandoned cutting the rest of the images. There were thirty-six separate images, each to be printed in five colors with a total of 550 sets produced, 99,000 separate printings were required. Rivière decided to translate the images into lithographs, and in 1902, *Les Trente-Six Vues de la Tour Eiffel* appeared. It was a collaboration of fellow artists and friends. The prologue was written by Arsène Alexandre, the art critic, the design and typography by Auriol, and the printing by Verneau. It was issued in an edition of 500, with an additional fifty deluxe sets. The work was loosely based on Hokusai's *Thirty-Six Views of Fujiyama*, and is one of the greatest examples of Japonisme. The combination of a Japanese style depicting an urban, technological, Western object makes it a perfect example of how French artists synthesized their Japanese influences.

"Quincan Grogne," watercolor, May 1907, 26x41 cm.

This period seems to have been the focal point for Rivière's career. By 1902 he had published several sets of lithographs, several books, and he had worked on woodcuts—most in the Japanese manner.

By 1902, sales of his work were declining and his work was changing stylistically. Yet Rivière seems not to have cared that he was no longer in vogue, and that outside of Verneau, he had no outlet for the sale of his works. He was still busy working on the murals for Hayashi's home and a similar commission for Verneau's house. And he was still active in the Oriental art circles and had formed a close friendship with Mme. Langweil and her daughter. By 1906 Rivière was working on a new series of lithographs with Verneau, *Au Vent de Noroit*, a set of eight, with four to appear in 1906, four in 1907, seemingly oblivious to the fact that sales were declining rapidly.

"Dans la Tour," lithograph, Les Trente-Six Vues de la Tour Eiffel, *no. 25, 1888-1902, 17x20 cm.*

"De la rue des Abbesses," lithograph, Les Trente-Six
Vues de la Tour Eiffel, *no. 19, 1888-1902, 17x20 cm.*

"Des Jardins du Trocadéro, l'automne," lithograph,
Les Trente-Six Vues de la Tour Eiffel, *no. 34, 1888-1902,*
17x20 cm.

Feelings and attitudes about art were changing rapidly in Paris now. The influence of Japonisme had given way to the Art Nouveau movement. The color revolution in printmaking in the 1890s was quickly losing practitioners and customers. Toulouse-Lautrec died and the romantic views of Montmartre disappeared from view. Montmartre itself had so declined into a mini-world of drugs, prostitution, and crime that few of its former habitues visited it.

In these early years of the 1900s, Rivière was in the process of changing his painting style. The direct influence of Japonisme was disappearing from his work. He was spending more time doing watercolors and less with lithography. While he must have been aware that he was gradually losing appeal and that, outside of Verneau, he had few outlets for his work, he did not seem to be concerned. As long as he remained active doing the work he enjoyed, fulfilling commissions given to him by Hayashi and Verneau, collecting Oriental art, and meeting with his select friends, Rivière seemed satisfied with his life.

It was within this environment that Rivière, over the next few years, would have to deal with a number of personal tragedies along with his self-imposed withdrawal from the Parisian art scene.

Rivière at work at Loguivy, c. 1904.

35

Italy and Books

1902-1921

RIVIERE suffered several setbacks and discouragements during 1905 and 1906. His close friend Hayashi had returned to Japan and died. They had been friends and collaborators for over ten years, and Hayashi's death affected Rivière deeply. Although he continued to collect Japanese art after Hayashi's death, it was no longer with the enthusiasm of previous years. He continued to acquire objects from Mme. Langweil and had even become "uncle to her daughter Berthe," but it was evident that with Hayashi's death Rivière's intense Japonisme ended. Then early in 1906 Verneau became ill and could no longer supervise his printing studio. Since the 1890s Verneau had been one of the leading printers of color lithographs and was the only one with whom Rivière had worked. Within a few months Verneau died, and Rivière had lost the friend and associate who had furthered his work more than anyone else. It was Verneau who had introduced Rivière to the opportunities lithography had to offer, and together they had produced Rivière's work over seventeen years. With the deaths of Hayashi and Verneau, Rivière lost both a spiritual, esthetic mentor and a technical, creative master. It was almost like losing one's inspiration and one's technique at once. After Verneau's death, Rivière did not create any new lithographic series, but he did finish the one series he had begun, *Le Beau Pays de Bretagne.* The series *Au Vent de Noroit,* however, was terminated. After his usual summer in Brittany in 1906, Rivière returned to etching after a sixteen-year lapse. He created scenes of Brittany printed in brown ink in small editions of twenty-five or so, and he printed the plates himself. It seemed that without Hayashi he was unable to continue in the Japanese

"Breton Coast," etching, edition of 25, 1911,
26.5x40 cm.

Verneau and his family

written by Georges Toudouze, an art critic and historian, and was designed by Auriol. Steinlen contributed the frontispiece portrait of Rivière. The book contained numerous color plates of his work as well as a list of all Rivière's graphic work and excerpts from various articles which had been written in recent years praising his work. However, little was said of Rivière's life. Practically nothing was mentioned about his parents, his childhood, or his marriage, and little was said about his Chat Noir days. Rivière worked closely with Toudouze on the book, and it appears he purposely left out most of the personal details, deciding instead to focus attention on his work. The book appeared at a time when Rivière was undergoing some difficulties, and perhaps it was as a result of the deaths of Hayashi and Verneau, perhaps because of a modest self image, or perhaps because he was no longer at the center of the Parisian art world that Rivière and Toudouze omitted the personal side of his life. Indeed, little is known of Rivière's activities from 1906 to 1911. In his memoirs, he omits completely these five years. He surely created etchings and watercolors during those years, as dates and places are noted on finished works. And the works themselves reveal a change—as they are predominantly religious scenes of churches and crosses, without people. In 1908 *The Studio* featured a lithograph by Rivière which he adapted from a watercolor he had done ten years earlier, but aside from this, he seems to have no other work published during this period.

style, and without Verneau he could no longer make lithographs. He continued to make etchings until 1913, creating about thirty-five images.

By 1907 Rivière's reputation was important enough for the art publisher Floury to commission a book about his life and works. It was

"View of Breton Village," etching, edition of 25,
1913, 26.5x40 cm.

"La Baie de Douarnenez," lithograph, from Le
Beau Pays de Bretagne, *no. 19, 1916, 23x35
cm.*

"Morgan," watercolor, 1916, 26x41 cm.

"Le vieux Moulin à Loguivy," lithographic
calendar, no. 13, 1910, 43x55 cm.

In 1911 Rivière returned to the art world.
Because of his continuing interest in ceramics,
which had since expanded beyond just Japanese
works, he approached Emile Levy, a proprietor of
an artbook shop, with the idea of preparing a book
on Muslim ceramics. Levy agreed, and the book
appeared as a history of the subject with numerous
photographic illustrations prepared by Rivière. With
his characteristic determination, Rivière had taught
himself the photographic process. He made
negatives and, with his charcteristic thoroughness,
made prints from them, insuring that the
reproductions in the book would be of the highest
quality. He was not satisfied to learn only part of a
technique; he learned it in its entirety, whether it
be woodcutting, lithography, or photography.
Another book, *Ceramics in Far Eastern Art*, was
published in 1913, and a work on Chinese ceramics
was planned.

In 1911 there appeared an article in *Art
and Decoration* by Monod-Herzen which described a
series of eight watercolors Rivière had completed,
all of the same image, painted at different times
throughout the day. Rivière was not entirely
neglected, and by 1913 when the Society of Wood
Engravers was planning a large exhibition, Rivière
was asked to participate with a group of his
woodcuts from the 1890s. The reaction to the show
as a whole was favorable, initiating a revival of
interest in the woodcut medium. Rivière himself
decided to create a new series of woodcuts, his
first since 1894. They were to be scenes of the only
trip he would ever take outside of France.

In 1911 Rivière's "niece" Berthe Langweil
was married to Andre Noufflard, a gentleman and
amateur painter. The couple invited the Rivières to
accompany them on a trip to Italy in 1913, where
they were to stay at the Noufflards' villa near
Florence and make side trips throughout the area
to view the art treasures from the Renaissance and
classical times. Mme. Rivière declined the

"Bois de Hetres à Kerzardern," lithographic
calendar, no. 20, 1917, 43x55 cm.

Andre and Berthe Noufflard

Rivière and Berthe Noufflard in Italy, 1913.

invitation, as Rivière said, "fearing long journeys," but he did go and the trip had a tremendous impact on him. He was able to see firsthand all of the works he had only seen in books, and he had the opportunity to sketch the images and places he admired. Rivière was an avid traveler and correspondent, writing his wife two to four postcards a day. And it was during this trip that he received word from Eugenie about her visit to an ophthalmologist, the first indication of the eye problems which were to become serious in later years.

Upon his return, Rivière spent the first part of 1914 completing the watercolors and woodcuts of his trip and making plans to exhibit them at the next woodcut show in the fall. He and Eugenie spent the summer in Brittany, at Morgat, and the work proceeded as usual, until word of the mobilization for war came. The little town was soon empty except for the Rivières and another couple. By September, Rivière and Eugenie decided to make the journey to Aix-les-Thermes, the place of his father's birth, where he had spent the years of the Franco-Prussian War. They returned to Paris in November, and Rivière completed work on a number of woodcuts of the Italian trip as well as finishing the printing of some woodcuts originally begun in 1891. These would be his last woodcuts.

During the First World War Rivière continued to work in watercolors, and in 1915 and 1916 he and Eugenie summered in Brittany. In 1917 and 1918 they spent their summers in Savoy with the Noufflards. Rivière began to experiment with tapestry and he continued his interest in photography.

Some of Rivière's old friends died during and just after the war, including Bing, Guneau, Grasset, and Degas, who passed away in the summer of 1917 while Rivière was in Brittany. He was especially saddened not to have been able to attend the funeral.

Rivière and his wife returned to Paris in October 1918 and in November, "we heard one fine morning, with what relief, the loud voice of the 'Savoyarde' accompanied by that of all the Paris bells to announce to us that the war was over and we had won. A poor victory which left us very low, very exhausted, but victory all the same!"

As life began to return to normal, Rivière enthusiastically resumed some of his literary and artistic activities. Demotte, a well-known antiquarian bookseller, asked Rivière to direct a publication which would reproduce the new acquisitions made each year at the Louvre. This he did, and it appeared over a three-year period until the death of Demotte caused the publication to cease. One of the three volumes issued was devoted exclusively to Degas and appeared in two parts in 1922 and 1923 under the title *Les Dessins de Degas Reproduite en Fac-Simile.* Rivière saw to it that the photoengravings were of the very highest quality, and had it not been for his embossed monogram on each plate, they might have been mistaken for originals. There were 100 reproductions, each in its own mat. Rivière also wrote the introduction, and the folio was issued in an edition of 250.

In 1920 Rivière was asked by the Museum of Decorative Arts to exhibit a series of watercolors which had never been shown before. Although Rivière "only wanted to show them to close friends," the exhibit took place during a three-week period in February 1921. The exhibit consisted of watercolors, etchings, and woodcuts. It was Rivière's last public exhibition. While some of the watercolors were recently completed, the etchings dated from 1906 to 1913, and the woodcuts from 1890 to 1894 as well as the last five done in 1914. In all, 209 pieces were shown: 151 watercolors, thirty etchings, twenty-eight woodcuts. Jean Laran, art historian and critic, wrote a review of the exhibit and spoke movingly of Rivière's artistic abilities. He discussed Rivière's philosophy of life, something which had not been presented to the public before. Rivière was "different from other current artists" because he was "not influenced by current times and fads." Laran compared him to Claude Lorraine and Millet, and described him as modest, honest, true, and just, in all, a complete artist. Rivière, at age fifty-seven, had become somewhat of an outsider to the art world, preferring instead to spend his time with his wife, Mme. Langweil, and the Noufflards. He willingly withdrew from public notice and created artworks without recognizing the trends of the times. By preference, he became a solitary artist.

Rivière worked on one last book, *Documents d'Art Chinois de la Collection Osvald Siren,* published in 1925. It was an illustrated documentation of the significant collection of Osvald Siren, the art historian and collector. Rivière wrote the section on Chinese ceramics.

During these last ten years, Rivière terminated work on woodcuts, etchings, and lithographs, only reluctantly allowing his work to be shown. He personally removed himself from the public eye. And yet, he was to live another thirty years. He would continue to create art and keep in touch with nature around him. He would try to maintain a reasonably stable life in the face of significant personal and political upheavals. That he succeeded was a testament to his personal strength and courage, his integrity, and his achievement.

Final Years
1921-1951

RIVIERE continued his friendships with the Noufflards, Jean Laran, and artists Pierre Louis Moreau and Andre Barbier. Rivière and Eugenie continued to summer in the country, with trips to the Noufflard estate in Normandy at Fresnay-le-Long. There were now two Noufflard daughters, Henriette and Genévieve. Rivière acted as their grandfather and remained as close as ever to the family.

While Rivière was always aware of the gradual loss of Eugenie's eyesight from glaucoma, the conditions worsened alarmingly at this time. They now spent their summers in Paris and their winters in Provence, at such places as Cassis, Bormes, Hyeres, Biot, and Mougins. Rivière enjoyed the new terrain and painted numerous watercolors. As he recalled, he was "able to return to the countryside to paint nature." But now Eugenie would accompany him, sitting beside him knitting while he painted and described to her the features of the countryside. In 1937 they found a small village to the north of Provence, Buis-le-Baronnies, which they liked very much. They resided in a small hotel and began to become acquainted with the villagers. By this time Eugenie was totally blind and Rivière had to take care of her and the household. It was a difficult time for him, but with her guidance he was able to maintain their comfortable life. Eugenie enjoyed playing the piano, and Rivière bought a phonograph and records of classical music. Every evening he would put on a concert for her and he observed "it was a great help to my wife's morale: when the concert was over, while I worked in my studio, I heard her trying on the piano to find again the tunes she had just listened to. . . ."

"Launay Mal Nomme', Bretagne," watercolor,
Sept. 1899

Rivière and Eugenie, c. 1930.

Rivière and Andre Noufflard

They returned to Buis-le-Baronnies each winter, and they arrived there in 1939 a few days before the country began to mobilize for war again. While Rivière was concerned about the impending war, he hoped they would be able to return to Paris at winter's end. For Rivière, it would be the third time in his life that France and Germany would be at war. In Buis-le-Baronnies they stayed at a hotel called *Fontaine d'Annibal*, which became crowded with people fleeing northern France. They met a couple named Fischer who had owned a photographic documentation shop in Paris, and the two couples became friendly, with Mme. Fischer often helping out the Rivières.

They also became friendly with a woman named Marcelle Schmiedler who was about Rivière's age and who was also spending the war years in Buis. She too helped Rivière care for Eugenie.

During the war years Rivière continued to go out into the countryside to paint, giving his work away to his friends. Mme. Jouselm, who owned the Fontaine d'Annibal, was the recipient of many watercolors from Rivière, some in lieu of rent.

In 1943 Eugenie suffered a dislocated thigh bone and had to remain in bed. When her leg became progressively more stiff, she was taken to the local hospital. She died in May and was buried in the village cemetery. Rivière and Eugenie had been together for fifty-five years, their only separation being Rivière's trip to Italy. Andre

"*Douarnenez,*" *watercolor, Aug. 1904*

*Rivière on his way to the day's painting site,
c. late 1930s.*

Noufflard came to take the despondent Rivière to
the Noufflards' new home in the Dordogne. As
Rivière adjusted to his circumstances, he began to
do watercolors again. In September, Andre was
able to return Rivière to Buis-le-Baronnies.

Rivière's friendship with Mme. Schmiedler
had grown to the point where he asked her to
marry him, but she refused. She instead returned
to her home in Lyons, and although she and
Rivière corresponded, they did not see one another
again. This was a difficult and unhappy time for
Rivière. He was alone and growing old, facing an
uncertain future.

By this time, German troops had invaded
the south of France, and to make matters worse,
brigands had taken over Rivière's hotel and forced
out all the occupants. Luckily, a room in a nearby
hotel was found for Rivière, but he was now
emotionally unable to work, although he persisted
in going out every day with his materials "to try."
At last, in August 1944, the town was liberated by
American soldiers and some order was restored.
Rivière was able to move back into the Fontaine
d'Annibal and he resumed his work with
enthusiasm. At eighty years of age, he was still
healthy and active.

In November 1944, while working on a
picture, Rivière found that he was having trouble
making out the details, the lines were fuzzy as if a
"thin mist was covering them." He realized he was
going blind and would no longer be able to paint.
Although he could see objects in general, he could

"Paris, Blvd. de Clichy," watercolor, Sept. 1934
(painted from Rivière's apartment window)

not focus on the finer details. He became depressed and forlorn. Once again, the Noufflards were there to help. Berthe Noufflard arrived to take him to an oculist in Paris, but he was so depressed and angry that he refused to go. He remained in Buis throughout the winter. Finally, when he returned to Paris in the spring, Berthe took him to a doctor. Rivière was diagnosed as having microscopic lesions on his retina. Although the doctor told him that the condition would not worsen, he knew he could not paint again.

Rivière stayed with the Noufflards until he could return to his old apartment. He returned to his studio, his possessions, his friends. "Each room, each piece of furniture, each object reminded me of sweet moments, when the dear companion of my life was still present. . . . I could see again all the beautiful objects collected for nearly fifty years and I could see them again, caress them and care for them: my books were also there with their countless pictures that my memory completed when they appeared a little cloudy to my failing eyes. . . . I have my good friends that I love and who love me, my very dear Berthe, my old Andre, more than a brother to me, my tender Henriette, my little godchild Genévieve . . . my good, faithful Barbier, I am surrounded by such cordial friendships, that I sometimes wonder how I could have deserved them. . . ."

*"Buis-le-Baronnies," watercolor, Aug. 1944
(Rivière's last watercolor, inscribed in lower
right, "to my old friend Andre")*

After his return to Paris, Rivière wrote his memoirs, dictating them to Mme. Fischer, a friend he met during the war years in Buis. On 24 August 1951 Rivière died at the age of eighty-seven. He had been cared for during his final months by the Noufflards at the home of Henriette in Sucy-en-Brie. He was buried at Fresnay-le-Long, the ancestral home of the Noufflards, and Eugenie was brought there and buried beside him. With this, Rivière's final wish was granted, for in the last paragraph of his memoirs he says, "Why would another little corner of the earth not offer us eternal rest? I would be happy then that it should be in the shade of the church at Fresnay, not far from the ancestral home of our very dear Noufflards. And the remains of my dear companion would come and join me there, where the sea wind chases the clouds above the verdant plains, hope of future harvests . . . nor would they forget the irises!"

Rivière working on his memoirs, c. 1946.

"Chantier de la Tour Eiffel," woodcut, 7 colors,
1889, 22x34.5 cm.

"Femme de la Garde-Guérin (St. Briac)," woodcut,
8 colors, from Paysages Bretons, no. 15,
1890, 23x35 cm.

"Baie de la Fresnaye (Saint-Caast)," woodcut, 8
colors, *from* Paysages Bretons, *no. 20, 1891,
23x35 cm.*

"Basilique d'Assise en Hiver," woodcut, 1914,
22x35 cm. (Riviere's last woodcut)

"Le Pardon de Sainte-Anne-la-Palud," woodcut,
5 sheets, 50 colors, from Paysages Bretons, *no.*
38, 1892, 34x114 cm.

"Etude de Vague," watercolor, June 1892,
22.5x34 cm.

"Le Bourg Dun," watercolor, May 1905,
22.5x34 cm.

"Sainte Marie du Menez Hom," watercolor, Aug.
1912, 22.5x34 cm.

"Buis-le-Baronnies," watercolor, Dec. 1939,
26x41 cm.

*"Le Coucher du Soleil," lithograph, 12 colors,
from* Les Aspects de la Nature, *no. 11, 1898,
54.5x83 cm.*

*"La Falaise," lithograph, 12 colors, from Les
Aspects de la Nature, no. 3, 1897, 54.5x83 cm.*

"Le Foret," lithograph, 12 colors, from Les
Aspects de la Nature, *no. 13, 1899, 54.5x83
cm.*

*"Paris vu de Montmartre," lithograph, 12
colors, from* Paysages Parisiens, *no. 2, 1900,
52.5x82 cm.*

*"L'Institut et la Cité," lithograph, 12 colors,
from* Paysages Parisiens, *no. 4, 1900, 52.5x82
cm.*

*"La Tempête," lithograph, 12 colors, from La
Féerie des Heures, no. 10, 1901, 24x60 cm.*

*"La Neige," lithograph, 12 colors, from La
Féerie des Heures, no. 14, 1902, 24x60 cm.*

"Bateaux au Mouillage à Treboul," lithograph,
12 colors, from Le Beau Pays de Bretagne, *no.
5, 1902, 23x35 cm.*

"Le Crépuscule," lithograph, 12 colors,
from La Féerie des Heures, *no. 12,
1902, 24x60 cm.*

"Lavoir à Treboul," lithograph, 14 colors, from Le Beau Pays de Bretagne, *no. 12, 1909, 23x35 cm.*

"Le Trieux à Kermarie," lithograph, 14 colors, from Le Beau Pays de Bretagne, *no. 15, 1912, 23x35 cm.*

*"Le Bois de Hetres à Kerzarden," lithograph, 14
colors, from* Le Beau Pays de Bretagne, *no. 20,
1917, 23x35 cm. (Rivière's last lithograph)*

"Le Port," lithograph, 15 colors, from Au Vent
de Noroit, *no. 1, 1906, 37.x5x49.5 cm.*

Books/Exhibition Brochures

Bibliography

Catalog Illustré de Estampe en Couleur de Henri Rivière. Paris: Eugene Verneau, 1905.

Cate, Phillip Dennis and Hitchings, Sinclair. *The Color Revolution.* Santa Barbara and Salt Lake City: Peregrine Smith Books, 1978.

Centenaire du Cabaret du Chat Noir. Paris: Musée de Montmartre, 1981.

Cochin, F. *Paul Signac.* Greenwich CT: New York Graphic Society, Ltd., 1971.

Exposition des Peintres-Graveurs. Paris: Durand-Ruel Gallery, 1889.

Exposition Henri Rivière: Aquarelles, Dessins et Gravures. Paris: Pavillon de Mars, Palais du Louvre, 1921.

Impey, Oliver. *Chinoiserie.* New York: Charles Scribner's Sons, 1977.

Ives, C.F. *The Great Wave.* New York: Metropolitan Museum of Art, 1974.

Japonisme in Art. An International Symposium. Edited by the Society for the Study of Japonisme. Tokyo: Committee for the Year 2001, 1980.

Julien, Philippe. *Montmartre.* New York: E.P. Dutton, 1977.

Julien, Philippe. *The Symbolists.* London: Phaidon Press, Ltd., 1973.

La March à l'Etoile, poeme et musique de Georges Fragerolle, dessins de Henri Rivière. Paris: Enoch Frères & Costallat, 1896, first edition.

Marx, Roger. *La Gravure Originale au XIXe Siècle.* Paris: Editions Aimery Somogy, 1962.

Mellerio, A. *La Lithographie en Couleurs.* Paris, 1898.

Moran, Louis. *French Illustrators.* New York: Charles Scribner's Sons, 1893.

Noufflard, Genévieve and Guyloë, Henriette. *André Noufflard, Berthe Noufflard, Leur Vie, Leur Peinture.* Imprimerie de la Vallée d'Eure, 1982.

Pont-Aven Catalog. 1977.

Rivière, Henri. *Les Dessins de Degas.* Paris: Demotte, 1922.

Articles / Periodicals

Rivière, Henri. *Les Trente-Six Vues de la Tour Eiffel.* Paris: Eugene Verneau, 1902.

Roman, J. *Paris, Fin de Siècle.* New York: Golden Griffin Books, Essential Encyclopedia Arts, Inc., 1960.

Rubenstein, Daryl R. *The Avant-garde in Theater & Art: French Playbills of the 1890s.* Washington DC: Smithsonian Institution Traveling Exhibition Service, 1973.

Sagot. *Catalogue d'Affiches Illustres Anciennes et Modern,* no. 30. Paris.

Sagot-Le Garrec Catalog, 1976.

Siren, Osvald. *Documents d'Art Chinois de la Collection Osvald Siren,* sous la direction de M. Henri Rivière. Paris and Brussells: G. von Oest, 1925.

Tinchant, A. *Serenites.* Paris, 1885.

Toudouze, Georges. *Henri Rivière: Peintre et Imagier.* Paris: Henri Fleury, 1907.

Weisberg, Gabriel. *Social Concern of the Worker: French Prints from 1830-1910.* Exhibition catalog. Salt Lake City: University of Utah, Utah Museum of Fine Arts, 1973.

Weisberg, Gabriel; Cate, Phillip Dennis, et al. *Japonisme—Japanese Influence on French Art 1854-1910.* London: Robert T. Sawyers Publications, 1975.

Whitford, Frank. *Japanese Prints and Western Painters.* New York: Macmillan, 1977.

Wichman, Siegfried. *Japonisme: The Japanese Influence on Western Art in the 19th and 20th Centuries.* New York: Harmony Books, 1981.

AD 42(Aug. 1972):467. Illustration.

"Beaux-Arts, Expositions à Paris." *Revue Encyclopaedique* (1892):1098-1102.

Bénédite, Léonce. "L'Exposition des Peintres-Graveurs." *Gazette des Beaux-Arts* (Mar. 1890):161-68.

Cate, Phillip Dennis. "Japanese Woodcuts and the Flowering of French Color Printmaking." *Artnews* 74(Mar. 1975):27-29.

Chicago Art Institute Scrapbook 12(Dec. 1899 to July 1900):142. Illustration.

Connoiseur 192(Jan. 1976):163. Gallerie d'Imagine exhibit, illustration.

Connoiseur 203(Jan. 1980):43. Illustration.

Frèrebeau-Oberthur, Mariel. "What is Montmartre? Nothing. What Should It Be? Everything!" *Artnews* 73(March 1977):60-62.

Gazette des Beaux-Arts, 1889.

Gazette des Beaux Arts 47(Jan.-Apr. 1956):111. Illustration.

Gusman, Pierre. "La Gravure sur bois en France au XIXe Siècle." *L'Académie des Beaux-Arts* (1929):204-206.

International Studio 49(Apr. 1913):131. Illustration.

"Journal of Paul Signac." *Arts de France,* 1947, no. 11 (1900-01); no. 17-19 (1902-09) and *Gazette des Beaux-Arts,* 1949 (1894-95); 1952 (1897-99); 1953 (1898-99).

Laran, J. "Henri Rivière." *L'Art et les Artistes* (Feb. 1921):178-85.

Leprieur, Paul. "L'Exposition des Peintres-Graveurs." *L'Artiste* (Apr. 1892):298-308.

de Lostalot, Alfred. "L'Exposition des Beaux-Arts." *Gazette des Beaux-Arts* (May 1892):416-21.

Mag Art 46(March 1953):114. Illustration.

Mag Art 46(March 1953):117. Illustration.

Marx, Roger. "L'Art à l'Ecole, l'Image Murale." *Revue: l'Enfant* 139.

Marx, Roger. "L'Exposition des Peintres-Graveurs." *L'Artiste* (Apr. 1893):286-92.

Monod-Herzen. "Le Ciels d'Henri Rivière." *Art et Decoration* 29(June 1911):197-200.

Mourney, Gabriel. "The Art of M. Henri Rivière as Expressed in His Chromo-Xylographs." *The Studio* 7(Mar. 1896):83-89.

Mourney, Gabriel. "The Illustration of Music." *The Studio* 15(Nov. 1898):86-98.

PCN 10(Mar. 1979):26. Illustration.

Reff, T. "Images of Flaubert's Queen of Sheba in Late 19th-Century Art." *Artist & Writer* (1974):126-33. Illustration.

Renault, Malo. "Henri Rivière." *Art et Decoration* 49(Feb. 1921):43-50.

Ritter, William. "Henri Rivière." *Die graphischen Künste.* 28(1899):107-122.

Rubin, William. "Shadows, Pantomimes and the Art of Fin-de-Siècle." *Magazine of Art* 46(Mar. 1953).

Sacs, Joan. "L'Art Extreme Oriental." (May 1914). Illustration.

Sarradin, Edouard. "Henri Rivière et son Oeuvre." *Art et Decoration* 3(1898):33-44.

"Société de Peintres-Graveurs Francais." *L'Image* (Apr. 1897).

Soulier, Gustave. "Nouvelles Estampes d'Henri Rivière." *Art et Decoration* 11(Jan. 1902):28-32.

Taylor, E.A. *The First Exhibition of the Society of Wood Engraving.* (1913):128-37. Illustration.

Catalog

**Theater productions at the
Chat Noir to which Riviere
contributed**

1888 La Tentation de St. Antoine, a
fairy story in 40 tableaux,
drawings by Henri Rivière,
music arranged by Albert
Tinchart

1890 *La Marche à L'Etoile,* mystery
play in 10 tableaux, drawings
by Henri Rivière, poetry and
music by Georges Fragerolle

1891 *Roland,* oratorio in 3 tableaux,
scenery by Henri Rivière, a
poem by Georges d'Esparbec,
music by Charles de Sivry

Phryné, Greek scenes in 7
tableaux, drawings by Henri
Rivière, poem by Maurice
Donnay, music by Charles de
Sivry

1892 *Ailleurs,* symbolic review in 2
parts and 20 tableaux,
drawings by Henri Rivière,
poem by Maurice Donnay,
music by Charles de Sivry

1893 *Sainte Genévieve de Paris,*
mystery play in 4 parts and 12
tableaux, drawings by Henri
Rivière, poems and music by
Leopold Dauphin and
Claudius Blanc

1894 *Hero et Leändre,* dramatic
poem in 3 acts and 20
tableaux, drawings by Henri
Rivière, poem by Edmond
Harancourt, music by Paul
and Lucien Hillemacher

Le Rêve de Zola, fantasy in 10
tableaux, drawings by J.
Depaquit, poem and music by
Jules Jouy, the last tableau
by Henri Rivière

1895 *L'Enfant Prodigue,* 6 tableaux,
drawings by Henri Rivière,
poetry and music by Georges
Fragerolle

1896 *Clairs de Lune,* fairy story in 6
tableaux, drawings by Henri
Rivière, poems and music by
Georges Fragerolle

Etchings:

Rivière completed about 35 etchings between 1906 and 1913. All were of the same size, 26.5 cm. x 40 cm. All were printed in brown ink, by the artist. A total of 25 images were printed for each edition, although some editions might have been less. Nearly all of the etchings were done in 5 or 6 states, but only the final state was printed in multiple impressions. Some prints would have Rivière's red initial monogram on them; some would have a red iris monogram on them; a few had both. Rivière would only sign the pieces in pencil if they were sold.

Watercolors:

All watercolors had a Rivière monogram on them. Most would indicate the place and the date of the completion of the watercolor. Only a very few watercolors were signed in pencil by Rivière.

Lithographs:

1889   "Paris en Hiver," 5 colors, program for the *Théatre Libre,* edition size unknown, printed by Verneau, 21.5 x 31.1 cm.

1890   "Boat on the Seine," 5 colors, program for the *Théatre Libre,* edition size unknown, printed by Verneau, 16 x 20 cm.

1893   "La Vague," 7 colors, from *L'Estampe Originale,* edition of 100, printed by Verneau, 29.2 x 45.7 cm.

1895   "Lavoir au Haut-Trestraou," 9 colors, from *Art et Décoration,* taken from woodcut (1891), edition size unknown, printed by Verneau, 15 x 23 cm.

"Le Village de la Chapelle (Saint Briac)," 7 colors, from *L'Art Décoratif,* vol. 8, taken from woodcut (1890), edition size unknown, printed by Verneau, 15 x 22.5 cm.

"L'Enfant Prodigue," 8 colors, announcement for the book of the same title, edition size unknown, printed by Verneau, 29 x 78 cm.

1896   "Le Bourg de Perros-Guirrec," 9 colors, from *The Studio,* March, VII, taken from woodcut (1891), edition size unknown, printed by Verneau, 14.5 x 23 cm.

"L'Hiver," (Image pour L'Ecole No. 1), 12 colors, edition of 1,000, printed by E. Marty, 57 x 85 cm.

"La Marche à l'Etoile," 8 colors, announcement for the book of the same title, edition size unknown, printed by Verneau, 29 x 78 cm.

"Clairs de Lune," 6 colors, announcement for the book of the same title, edition size unknown, printed by Verneau, 29 x 78 cm.

"Le Juif Errant," 8 colors, announcement for the book of the same title, edition size unknown, printed by Verneau, 29 x 78 cm.

1897 *Les Aspects de la Nature*
Series of 16 in 12 colors. Each was done in an edition of 1,000 plus 25 on chine numbered and signed by the artist, printed by Verneau, 54.5 x 83 cm. Numbers 1 through 6 were published in 1897; numbers 7 through 12 were published in 1898; numbers 13 through 16 were published in 1899.

1. "La Baie"
2. "Nuit en Mer"
3. "La Falaise"
4. "La Montagne"
5. "Soir d'Eté"
6. "Le Fleuve"

1898 *Les Aspects de la Nature*
(series)
7. "L'ile"
8. "Le Crépuscle"
9. "Le Bois, L'Hiver"
10. "Le Lever de la Lune"
11. "Le Coucher du Soleil"
12. "Le Ruisseau"

*Le Beau Pays de Bretagne**
Series of 20 in 12 or 14 colors. Each was done in an edition of 500, plus 100 which were numbered and signed by the artist, 23 x 35 cm. One edition was printed each year from 1898 to 1917.

1. "Départ de Bateaux à Tréboul"

Le Beau Pays de Bretagne—Calendars
(series)
Series of 12 in 12 or 14 colors. Each was done in an edition of 1,000, typography and printing by Auriol, 43 x 55 cm. Each calendar edition was printed and published at the same time as the lithograph.

1. "Départ de Bateaux à Tréboul"

"Les Femmes," 4 colors from *The Studio,* November, XV, taken from *La Marche à l'Etoile,* edition size unknown, printed by Verneau, 14 x 20.5 cm.

"Clairs de Lune," 5 colors, from *The Studio,* November, XV, taken from poster, edition size unknown, printed by M. Enoch et Cie, 8 x 21.5 cm.

"La Clairière," 12 colors, announcement for *Les Aspects de la Nature,* edition size unknown, printed by Verneau, 90 x 122 cm.

1899 *Les Aspects de la Nature*
(series)
13. "Le Foret"
14. "La Plage"
15. "Le Hameau"
16. "La Mer"

Le Beau Pays de Bretagne
(series)

2. "Rue à Tréboul"

Le Beau Pays de Bretagne-Calendars (series)

2. "Rue à Tréboul"

1900 *Paysages Parisiens*

Series of 8 in 12 colors. Each was done in an edition of 1,000 plus 25 on chine numbered and signed by the artist, printed by Verneau, 52.5 x 82 cm. All were published in 1900.

1. "L'Ile des Cygnes"
2. "Paris Vu de Montmartre"
3. "Quai d'Austerlitz"
4. "L'Institut et la Cité"
5. "Les Fortifications"
6. "Le Pont des Saints-Pères et le Louvre"
7. "Du Haut des Tours Notre-Dame"
8. "Le Trocadéro"

Le Beau Pays de Bretagne (series)

3. "Clair de Lune à Landmélus"

Le Beau Pays de Bretagne-Calendars (series)

3. "Clair de Lune à Landmélus"

1901 *La Féerie des Heures*

Series of 16 in 12 colors. Each was done in an edition of 1,000 plus 25 on chine numbered and signed by the artist, printed by Verneau, 24 x 60 cm. Numbers 1 through 8 were published in 1901; numbers 9 through 16 were published in 1902.

1. "L'Aube"
2. "Le Soleil Couchant"
3. "L'Arc-en-Ciel"
4. "La Brume"
5. "Le Premier Quartier"
6. "Les Reflets"
7. "L'Averse"
8. "Le Vent"

"Le Soir," 12 colors, announcement for *La Féerie des Heures,* edition size unknown, printed by Verneau, 24 x 60 cm.

Le Beau Pays de Bretagne (series)

4. "Ruisseau à Lopérec"

Le Beau Pays de Bretagne-Calendars (series)

4. "Ruisseau à Lopérec"

1902 *La Féerie des Heures* (series)

9. "La Pleine Lune"
10. "La Tempête"
11. "Le Calme Plat"
12. "Le Crépuscle"
13. "L'Orage qui Monte"
14. "La Neige"
15. "La Nuit"
16. "Les Derniers Rayons"

Le Beau Pays de Bretagne (series)

5. "Bateau au Mouillage à Tréboul"

Le Beau Pays de Bretagne-Calendars (series)

5. "Bateau au Mouillage à Tréboul"

Les Trente-Six Vues de la Tour Eiffel, 36 lithographs, 5 colors, edition of 500 numbered and signed plus 50 deluxe roman numeraled and signed in pencil, designed by Auriol, printed by Verneau, 17 x 20 cm.

1. "Frontispice"
2. "Les Chantiers de la Tour Eiffel"
3. "La Tour en Construction Vue du Trocadéro"
4. "En Haut de la Tour"
5. "Rue Bethoveen"
6. "Des Jardins Maraîchers des Grenelle"
7. "Du Pont des Saints-Pères"
8. "Du Quai de la Conférence"
9. "De Notre-Dame"
10. "Du Boulevard de Clichy"
11. "Du Point-du-Jour"
12. "Fête sur la Seine le 14 Juillet"
13. "Du Quai de Passy"
14. "De la Rue Lamarck"
15. "De la Rue Rochechouart"
16. "Du Quai de Passy par la Pluie"
17. "En Bateau-Mouche"
18. "Du Quai de Grenelle"
19. "De la Rue des Abbesses"
20. "Du Pont de Grenelle"
21. "Sur les Toits"
22. "Du Bois de Boulogne"
23. "De la Place de la Concorde"

24. "De l'Ile des Cygnes"
25. "Dans la Tour"
26. "Du Pont d'Austerlitz"
27. "Derrière l'Elan de Frémiet (Trocadéro)"
28. "Du Quai de Javel (Baraque d'Aguilleur)"
29. "Du Bas-Meudon Vieux Lavoir"
30. "Ouvrier Plombier dans la Tour"
31. "Du Quai de Passy Charbonniers"
32. "De la Gare du Bas-Meudon"
33. "De l'Estacade"
34. "Des Jardins du Trocadéro, l'Automne"
35. "Les Péniches"
36. "Le Peintre dans la Tour"

1903 *Le Beau Pays de Bretagne* (series)

6. "Les Bords du Trieux au Crépuscule"

Le Beau Pays de Bretagne-Calendars (series)

6. "Les Bords du Trieux au Crépuscule"

1904 *Le Beau Pays de Bretagne* (series)

7. "Loguivy le Soir"

Le Beau Pays de Bretagne-Calendars (series)

7. "Loguivy le Soir"

1905 *Le Beau Pays de Bretagne* (series)

8. "Le Port de Loguivy à Marée Basse"

Le Beau Pays de Bretagne-Calendars (series)

8. "Le Port de Loguivy à Marée Basse"

1906 *Au Vent de Noroit*
Series of 4 in 12 or 15 colors. Each was done in an edition of 1,000 plus 25 on chine numbered and signed by the artist, printed by Verneau, 37.5 x 49.5 cm. All were published in 1906.

1. "Le Port"
2. "Le Travail aux Champs"
3. "Les Mousses"
4. "Les Vieux"

Announcement for *Au Vent de Noroit*, 8 colors, edition size unknown, printed by Verneau, 23 x 60 cm.

Le Beau Pays de Bretagne (series)
9. "Arrivée de Bateaux à Tréboul"

Le Beau Pays de Bretagne-Calendars (series)
9. "Arrivée de Bateaux à Tréboul"

1907 *Le Beau Pays de Bretagne* (series)
10. "La Première Etoile. Landiris"

Le Beau Pays de Bretagne-Calendars (series)
10. "La Première Etoile. Landiris"

1908 "Matin de Brume à Loguivy," 7 colors, edition of 100, printed by *The Studio*, 20 x 32.5 cm.

Le Beau Pays de Bretagne (series)
11. "La Balise sur le Trieux (Le Phare)"

Le Beau Pays de Bretagne-Calendars (series)
11. "La Balise sur le Trieux (Le Phare)"

1909 *Le Beau Pays de Bretagne* (series)
12. "Lavoir à Tréboul"

Le Beau Pays de Bretagne-Calendars (series)
12. "Lavoir à Tréboul"

1910 *Le Beau Pays de Bretagne* (series)
13. "Le Vieux Moulin à Loguivy"

Le Beau Pays de Bretagne-Calendars (series)
13. "Le Vieux Moulin à Loguivy"

1911 *Le Beau Pays de Bretagne* (series)

14. "Le Port de Douarnenez"

Le Beau Pays de Bretagne-Calendars (series)
14. "Le Port de Douarnenez"

1912 *Le Beau Pays de Bretagne* (series)
15. "Le Trieux à Kermarie"

Le Beau Pays de Bretagne-Calendars (series)
15. "Le Trieux à Kermarie"

1913 *Le Beau Pays de Bretagne* (series)
16. "L'ile de Bréhat"

Le Beau Pays de Bretagne-Calendars (series)
16. "L'ile de Bréhat"

1914 *Le Beau Pays de Bretagne* (series)
17. "Le Port de Ploumanach"

Le Beau Pays de Bretagne-Calendars (series)
17. "Le Port de Ploumanach"

Woodcuts

1915   *Le Beau Pays de Bretagne*
        (series)
        18. "Brume en Mer"

        *Le Beau Pays de
        Bretagne-Calendars*
        (series)
        18. "Brume en Mer"

1916   *Le Beau Pays de Bretagne*
        (series)
        19. "La Baie de Douarnenez"

        *Le Beau Pays de
        Bretagne-Calendars*
        (series)
        19. "La Baie de Douarnenez"

1917   *Le Beau Pays de Bretagne*
        (series)
        20. "Le Bois de Hetres à
            Kerzardern"

        *Le Beau Pays de
        Bretagne-Calendars*
        (series)
        20. "Le Bois de Hetres à
            Kerzardern"

*Proofs from these series have been personally annotated and signed by Rivière, beyond the normal edition sizes.

Note: A number of woodcuts were made into lithographs and included in the publication of articles about Rivière in magazines like *The Studio, L'Art Décoratif, Art et Décoration*:

"Lavoir au Haut-Trestraou," from *Art et Décoration,* 1895, taken from woodcut 1891, printed by Verneau, 15 x 23 cm.

"Le Village de la Chapelle (St. Briac)," from *L'Art Décoratif,* vol. 8, 1895, taken from woodcut 1890, printed by Verneau, 15 x 22.5 cm.

"Le Bourg de Perros-Guirrec," from *The Studio,* March 1896, taken from woodcut 1891, printed by Verneau, 14.5 x 23 cm.

All woodcuts were printed in editions of 20, although some additional proofs do exist. The woodcuts made from 1889 to 1894 have Rivière's red initial monogram on them. The woodcuts made in 1914 may or may not bear the monogram. Some woodcuts were signed in pencil by Rivière. It is believed that he signed those that were sold. All woodcuts were printed by the artist on hand-made, 100-year-old Japanese paper.

Two woodcuts, completed for the 36 Views series, were done in only three copies, and all were pencil signed by the artist.

Paysage Bretons
23 x 35 cm. editions of 20 plus proofs, wood burned after printing*

I. "Lancieux (St. Briac)," 8 woodblocks, 1890

II. "Les Balises: La Bouche, Chéruette et l'Ane (St. Briac) au Crépuscule," 5 woodblocks, 1890

III. "Le Béchet (St. Briac)," 5 woodblocks, 1890

IV. "Femmes Séchant du Linge (St. Briac)," 6 woodblocks, 1890

V. "Le Perron (St. Briac)," 6 woodblocks, 1890

VI. "Vaches dans les Champs de la Garde-Guérin (St. Briac)," 8 woodblocks, 1890

VII. "La Garde-Guérin (St. Briac)," 8 woodblocks, 1890

VIII. "La Pointe de la Haye (St. Briac)," 8 woodblocks, 1890

IX. "La Balise Chéruette à Marée Basse (St. Briac)," 9 woodblocks, 1890

X. "Potager à la Ville-Hue (St. Briac)," 8 woodblocks, 1890

XI. "L'Heure du Pain à la Ville-Hue (St. Briac)," 8 woodblocks, 1890

XII. "Barque et Steam-Boat (St. Briac)," 8 woodblocks, 1890

XIII. "Les Ebihiens (St. Briac)," 8 woodblocks, 1890

XIV. "Un Cheval et le Village de la Chapelle (St. Briac)," 7 woodblocks, 1890

XV. "Femme de la Garde-Guérin (St. Briac)," 8 woodblocks, 1890

XVI. "Une Femme et une Vache Pointe de la Haye (St. Briac)," 8 woodblocks, 1890

XVII. "Le Village de la Chapelle Vu des Tertres (St. Briac)," 7 woodblocks, 1890

XVIII. "Pointe de la Haye Vue de la Garde-Guérin (St. Briac)," 7 woodblocks, 1890

XIX. "Un Grain (St. Briac)," 8 woodblocks, 1890

"La Pointe du Décolle (St. Briac)," 10 woodblocks, woodblocks prepared in 1891 but printed in 1914

"Pêcheurs en Mer (St. Briac)," 8 woodblocks, woodblocks prepared in 1891 but printed in 1914

XX. "Baie de la Fresnaye (St. Caast)," 8 woodblocks, 1891

XXI. "Le Chatelier et le Fort Lalatte (St. Caast)," 8 woodblocks, 1891

XXII. "Barque, Baie de la Fresnaye (St. Caast)," 11 woodblocks, 1891

XXIII. "Ar-Frich (Ploumanac'h)," 5 woodblocks, 1891

XXIV. "Église Notre-Dame de la Clarté (Ploumanac'h)," 10 woodblocks, 1891

XXV. "Plateau de la Clarté (Ploumanac'h)," 10 woodblocks, 1891

XXVI. "Le Bourg de Perros-Guirrec," 9 woodblocks, 1891

XXVII. "Cimetière et Église de Perros-Guirrec," 10 woodblocks, 1891

XXVIII. "Enterrement à Trestraou," 12 woodblocks, 1891

XXIX. "Lavoir au Haut-Trestraou," 9 woodblocks, 1891

XXX. "Gabares Devant l'ile à Bois (Loguivy)," 9 woodblocks, 1891

XXXI. "Homardier à l'Embouchure du Trieux (Loguivy)," 9 woodblocks, 1891

XXXII. "L'Embouchure du Trieux (Loguivy)," 12 woodblocks, 1891

XXXIII. "Baie de Launay (Loguivy)," 11 woodblocks, 1891

XXXIV. "Vanneuses (Loguivy)," 12 woodblocks, 1891

XXXV. "Femme Ramassant des Aiguilles de Pins (Bords du Trieux-Loguivy)," 10 woodblocks, 1891

XXXVI. "Bois de Pins à Kermarie (Loguivy)," 11 woodblocks, 1891

XXXVII. "Petit Bois au Béret (Douarnenez)," 11 woodblocks, 1892-93

XXXVIII. "Le Pardon de Sainte-Anne-la-Palud," 5 sheets, 34 x 114 cm., 50 woodblocks (10 colors), 1892-93

XXXIX. "Départ de Sardiniers à Tréboul," 12 woodblocks, 1893-94

XXXX. "Lavoir sous Bois à Loguivy," 3 sheets, 34 x 67 cm., 30 woodblocks (10 colors), 1894

"Lendemain de Tempête, Baie de Launay (Loguivy)," 10 woodblocks, woodblocks prepared and printed in 1914

"Le Fossoyeur (Tréboul)," 12 woodblocks, woodblocks prepared and printed in 1914

La Mer: Etudes de Vagues
23 x 35 cm., editions of 20 plus proofs, woods burned after printing

I. "Vague par la Pluie (Port-Hue-St.Briac)," 6 woodblocks, 1890

II. "Petite Vague Montante (Pointe de la Haye)," 6 woodblocks, 1890

III. "Vague Mer Montante (Plage de la Garde-Guérin)," 6 woodblocks, 1890

IV. "Vague Mer Descendante (Chenal de l'ile Tristan)," 5 woodblocks, 1892

V. "L'Écume après la Vague (Tréboul)," 5 woodblocks, 1892

VI. "Coup de Vent—La Vague Vient de Taper et Retombe en Cascade—(Tréboul)," 7 woodblocks, 1892

"Vague Frappant Contre le Rocher et Retombant en Arceau," 6 woodblocks, woodblocks prepared and printed in 1914

Planches Hors Série
"Chantier de la Tour Eiffel," edition of 20, 22 x 34.5 cm., 7 woodblocks, 1889

"L'Enterrement aux Parapluies," 24.5 x 34.5 cm., 6 woodblocks, woodblocks prepared in 1891, 10 printed in 1891 and 10 printed in 1914

Two "plates" for the *36 Views of the Eiffel Tower:* 4 colors, printed by the artist, editions of 3, signed in pencil, 17 x 20 cm.

I. "Du Viaduc d'Auteuil," 17 x 20 cm., editions of 3 plus proofs, 4 woodblocks, 1891

II. "Du Pont d'Austerlitz," 17 x 20 cm., editions of 3 plus proofs, 4 woodblocks, 1891

"La Basilique d'Assise en Hiver," 21.5 x 35.5 cm., editions of 20 plus proofs, 12 woodblocks, 1914

*A number of woodblocks still exist in Rivière's estate collection and at the Bibliotechque Nationale.

Rivière states in his memoirs that a number of woodblock editions prepared in 1890 were only partially printed, half of them for a Durand-Ruel exhibit in 1891, the other half not printed until 1914. However, we do not know to which ones he was specifically referring.

In a book written by Louis Moran in 1898, *Quelque Artistes de ce Temps,* he says that Rivière intended to do 100 images in the *Paysages Bretons* series but completed only 40 and that Rivière intended to do 33 images in the *La Mer* series but "accounted" for only 14.

At the time of this writing, only 10 images for the *Eiffel Tower* series were complete, but he gives no indication whether they were woodblocks or some other medium.

Moran also refers to another series, *La Seine,* that Rivière was supposedly working on, of which only 2 or 3 images were complete out of a prepared 50.

There are a number of unfinished images of woodblocks available today. They appear to have been in preparation during the 1890 to 1893 period of the *Paysage Bretons* series. They are not named or numbered. Rivière does not speak of any unfinished pieces, nor does he mention anything about the possible number completed for each of his series.

The Rivière art works are in the
process of becoming a gift to the
Jane Voorhees Zimmerli Art
Museum, Rutgers University,
State University of New Jersey,
a gift of Armond and Sara Fields.

Afterword

Rivière had a profound and insightful attitude towards collecting and collectors. As he states in his memoirs:

"People have often made jokes about collectors and have even treated them as faddists. Faddists, yes, those who indiscriminately accumulate objects to make a set, etc. And yet! Sometimes they then amass a series of documents that can serve some historian enamored with details. But the man who can see, choose, and understand, who loves the beauty of any work of art, he is not a faddist, he is an enthusiast and he can save many things, which, but for him, would disintegrate in the dust of an attic, would fall to pieces in a dumping ground or be melted by some recuperator of precious metals.

"For the real collector, 'objects d'art' are not lifeless things, as the vulgar herd thinks; they live a mute but eloquent existence just the same and the person who possesses them brings them to life with his deep affection for them. And they are surely happy to be well cared for, well presented, and to see themselves often looked at, to feel themselves pressed by pious hands, which only handle them with care. Thus, they share the existence of their possessor, share his daily life, like good friends, ever present and never tired of being admired.

"Let us not joke too much about collectors; let us look at them rather, training their talents as hunters, their flair as connoisseurs, and let us share their joy for an unexpected find!"

This writer became a collector of Rivière's work and of his life experiences, as well. By sharing them with the reader, I hope that they have been brought to life and examined.

Rivière became my good friend, and I share the joy of having known him.

Index